Babes In The Jungle

A Year of Village Life in the Niger Delta

by
David Clark

Bloomington, IN Milton Keynes, UK

authorHOUSE®

AuthorHouse™
1663 Liberty Drive, Suite 200
Bloomington, IN 47403
www.authorhouse.com
Phone: 1-800-839-8640

AuthorHouse™ UK Ltd.
500 Avebury Boulevard
Central Milton Keynes, MK9 2BE
www.authorhouse.co.uk
Phone: 08001974150

First published by AuthorHouse 9/12/2006

ISBN: 1-4259-5848-6 (sc)

Printed in England

This book is printed on acid-free paper.

For my extended family

Table of Contents

Chapter 1
The Voyage

Our departure from England was not entirely smooth. Some friends invited us to their home for a delicious lunch of chicken followed by strawberries. Then we left the house in Enfield that we had been renting for several months and our friends took us into London to spend our last night in England at a hotel near Euston Station which had better remain nameless.

This was July 1965, well before the days when en suite bathrooms were the rule rather than the exception. I went down the corridor to the bathroom to run the bath then returned to our room to fetch something or other. Unfortunately the rate of flow of water from the bath taps was considerably faster than we were used to, and when I got back to the bathroom, the water was already running over the top of the bath on to the floor, though it had not yet betrayed its presence by emerging under the door. There was no overflow outlet from the bath, though there was at least a drain in the floor. So there followed a few frantic moments of furtive mopping up, and hoping that the water had not penetrated the ceiling of the floor below.

Happily none of the hotel staff appeared while all this was going on. Eventually the situation was brought under control with nothing worse than a pair of wet socks. With practice we managed to run the bath less disastrously until not only I but also my wife Glenys and our 16-month old baby Helen were all sufficiently clean.

Once Helen was asleep, Glenys and I went down to the restaurant to enjoy our evening meal of more chicken followed by more strawberries. I celebrated with a glass of cider, and Glenys celebrated by dropping her chicken on the floor. We were not sorry to retire fairly early, though after all our efforts of planning and packing, we were both excited at the months in Africa that lay ahead of us. I was a post-graduate student at the London School of Oriental and African Studies (SOAS), and was to do linguistic field work on a hitherto unwritten language called Ekpeye, spoken in what was in those days known as the Eastern Region of Nigeria. Glenys was qualified as a medical doctor, but also had some training in linguistics, and was intending to help me as much as possible rather than focus on medicine. Helen, though she did not know it, was to help us form relationships with the people we would live among.

Next morning we took a taxi to Euston Station for the boat train to Liverpool, reserved for passengers on the Elder Dempster Lines ship the MV Accra. A couple more friends came to the station to help us, one of them a former fellow-student from Nigeria, Amos Udonsak by name. No doubt after four years in England he would have loved to be coming with us. The journey passed smoothly, with Helen falling asleep in the dining car. The problems began when we got out of the train and were in the queue to go up the gangway and board the ship. The shipping line had made it very clear that there were no facilities on board for washing nappies, and people with babies and small children were expected to bring their own supply of disposable nappies to meet all their needs. So among the things we were carrying was a very large and unwieldy plastic bag filled with two weeks' stockpile of disposable nappies.

Just as we got near the bottom of the gangway, the bag burst, and the nappies cascaded onto the quay. What to do? We rounded them up as best we could, but the state of the bag was now such that the person carrying it needed both arms to restrain the wayward contents, and could not carry anything else. If we were all three to board at once, then neither parent would have a hand free to hold Helen. At 16 months she was a fairly steady walker, but we did not feel like letting her lurch up the steep gangway unaided, and risk falling off it either onto the quay below, or worse, into the water. We could hardly leave our goods on the quay, especially the essential nappies, which might well have blown away.

Help materialised in the form of a genial lady who was asking the boarding passengers questions from a form that she was filling up. She offered to hold Helen's hand while we took the baggage on board, an offer we gladly accepted. This meant that she could not fill up any more forms till one of us got back. So Glenys and I went up the gangway, thinking to drop our things quickly in our cabin and return for our precious daughter. But the ship was larger than either of us had realised, and it took longer than we expected to find the cabin, which turned out to be at the other end of the ship. I quickly rushed back to the top of the gangway, only to find I was on the wrong deck, and the access was on the deck above. I could see the poor questionnaire lady still faithfully clutching Helen's hand, and looking increasingly desperate as the queue of potential questionees got shorter and shorter. Eventually I managed to find the right deck and retrieve Helen, who had accepted our temporary separation quite placidly. Despite my profuse thanks for her help, the lady with the questionnaires was a little less genial than she had been. With hindsight, we should have stopped at the top of the gangway and gone back immediately, but it was our first time on such a large ship, and we had no appreciation of its size and complexity.

My parents had made a day trip to Liverpool from their home in Bristol to see us off, and once the passengers were all safely on board, the visitors were allowed to join them and look over the ship. Before the ship sailed, there were ample warnings over the loudspeaker system that the visitors should disembark, and by this time we knew exactly where the gangway was, and made sure the parents left in good time. Only from the perspective of forty years later can we appreciate what they must have felt like to see their one and only granddaughter disappearing for over a year to a destination that was even further beyond their imagination than it was beyond ours. But for us at the time it was all a big and eagerly anticipated adventure.

The meal system on board was that small children had to eat separately from adults and to be supervised by their parents. They were then confined to the nursery so that the adult meals were not disturbed by howling tinies. This was obviously to the advantage of the adults without children, though it made meal times last twice as long for the parents. But it worked well enough. On the train we had made the acquaintance of a Mrs. Haylock who was travelling to Ghana, and we had our first evening meal with her, at which we all filled up request slips for permanent dining room seating. We knew nobody else on board so since we were going to be spending a year living among Africans, we requested the company of Africans at dinner.

About nine in the evening the Mersey pilot was put off the ship into a small launch at Holyhead, and so was another man. We learned that this was a well-wisher who had apparently ignored all the warnings to leave the ship before it sailed, and had suffered the consequences. The sea was choppy, and before the eyes of many interested onlookers, this clown got quite a soaking before making it safely into the launch. His only consolation was a few ironic cheers from the passengers. Anglesey was the last land we were to see for several days.

Life on board was luxurious and lazy, but fortunately for me, we were spared rough weather crossing the Bay of Biscay. Glenys, whose stomach is a lot steadier than mine when it comes to travel, was secretly a little regretful at missing the chance to show her aplomb in such circumstances. There were awkward swells from time to time that swished the water in the ship's swimming pool alarmingly from side to side, but the worst that came of the pitching and tossing was being involuntarily turned over in your bunk at night. But this was more than offset by the novelty and beauty of the surroundings. The seascapes and skyscapes offered endless variety, especially once we got far enough south to see the shoals of flying fish. The sea colour was green as long as we were over the continental shelf, but once we left it and entered the deep ocean, it changed to blue. This was not just a reflection of the sky, as it persisted even when there were clouds overhead. One experience I enjoyed every evening was standing at the stern and watching the ship's wake, with the ever changing iridescence of the churning water.

When we saw our dining room seating, we found we were on a table of four with two British women, both married to Africans. They formed an interesting and sobering contrast. Jean was a physiotherapist from Scotland, married to a doctor from Nigeria. She had already lived for several years in Nigeria, and had two girls aged about eight and five. They all understood at least some Yoruba, the language of their father. Jean was returning from leave and knew exactly what kind of situation she was going to, a situation to which she had already made a good adjustment.

The other woman was married to a Ghanaian engineer, and also had a daughter of about eight. She had met and married her husband in England and was going to Africa for the first time. She seemed to be utterly unaware of the huge differences she would face, and to have made no effort to find out about them or prepare for them. For instance when I asked her what language her husband spoke, she looked completely blank and replied, "Well, African I suppose." The possibility that there might be more than one language spoken in Africa had obviously never occurred to her. How she eventually coped with African reality we never discovered, but the omens were not good. At least her daughter seemed to be more intelligent than she was, so maybe the child was able to adapt better.

7

When we looked around the dining room, we were astonished and rather horrified to observe that there were no tables with both Europeans and Africans sitting together. Our request to sit with Africans had apparently broken some unwritten rule, and European women married to Africans was evidently the nearest that was permitted. We never encountered any overt racial prejudice among the other passengers, so could only conclude that the de facto colour bar was company policy. Mrs. Haylock, for what reason she never divulged, was among the privileged élite invited to dine at the captain's table. She was quite devoid of social snobbery, and took a perverse delight in introducing us small fry to the other top table passengers when an opportunity arose. They never appeared to resent it.

The first landfall was at Las Palmas in the Canary Islands. After breakfast we left Helen in the nursery and went ashore with Jean and her two girls. By this time the weather was warm enough for me to be wearing shorts. Jean's younger girl looked me up and down with a disapproval that was as obvious as the Fife accent in her comment, "Och, ye've got hair all doon your legs." But she was still willing to spend the morning in the company of the hairy beast.

This was in the days before the arrival of the Jumbo Jet and mass tourism. The quay was lined with taxi drivers anxious to take passengers around the island, and especially its shops. Jean had been in Las Palmas before, and knew that the sensible thing to do was to ignore the taxis at the head of the queue because the further you walked down the queue, the lower the price you could bargain. We eventually came to an agreement with a driver and set off. Outnumbered by womenfolk, I had to endure a certain amount of shopping before we set off on a sightseeing tour, though even I was glad to buy a straw hat as protection from the sun. We went up a very steep circular road to the top of a conical peak overlooking an extinct volcano crater called the Caldera de Bandama. From there we could see a good deal of the island despite the cloud draped around the tops of other mountains. Apart from some vineyards and banana plantations, the island was more barren than we had expected, and we felt no desire to spend a holiday there. By noon we were back on board the ship and off on the next leg of the journey.

There was plenty of organised entertainment on board, though with Helen to care for, we did not attend evening functions very often. On the Sunday we spent at sea there was a church service conducted by the captain at which Glenys played the dilapidated piano for the hymns. In talking to other passengers we had discovered several who were intending to learn one African language or another, so I offered to give some classes in basic phonetics, and had a small but fairly regular group attending. Whether it helped them later on I have no idea, but it was good practice for me. There were also various sports activities, in some of which we participated, though with a conspicuous lack of success.

The next stop was at Freetown, Sierra Leone. Among the ship's passengers were the Prime Minister of Sierra Leone, Sir Albert Margai, and his entourage. A couple of days before we reached Freetown, he had in his official capacity given a cocktail party for all the other passengers. Later that day there was a fancy dress dinner, and we had enjoyed seeing him showing his human side by wearing a paper hat and playing with a balloon.

When we woke up in Freetown, it was to an unaccustomed din. On the quay there was a large welcome party in traditional dress for Sir Albert, and the crowd kept up a display of singing and dancing for three hours. Apart from a military guard of honour and a naval band, there was a variety of traditional instruments that we could not identify. The Prime Minister went ashore soon after nine o'clock, and by about ten, peace was restored.

While Helen was having her morning sleep, we took advantage of the opportunity to take a short tour of Freetown, visiting the Parliament House, the museum, a folk crafts centre, and a beach. This was the first time either of us had set foot on African soil, a pleasant and memorable way of marking my 28th birthday. We were left with two contrasting impressions. First there was the beauty of the setting among rugged hills covered in thick vegetation made up of numerous unfamiliar trees. We marvelled at the exotic flowers in bloom, the lizards scampering around the grounds of the Parliament, and the huge dragonflies zooming and hovering here and there. But we could not fail to see also the vast difference between the living standards of the local people and those of the expatriate community. The local people lived mainly in overcrowded houses made of wood or corrugated iron. Even the main street (Oxford Street!) was not sealed. The expatriates lived in detached bungalows on the hills outside the town and near the beach. We had to wonder why more had not been done during the colonial period to provide better facilities for the majority population, at least those in the easily accessible urban areas.

But we were also parents with mundane concerns, and the tour lasted longer than we had been led to expect. We began to get anxious in case Helen woke before we returned and found herself alone in the cabin, but happily she was still sound asleep when we got back. Departure from Freetown was delayed by the morning's festivities, but the afternoon was beguiled by some Africans in canoes paddling around the ship. Passengers would throw coins into the clear water and the canoeists would dive overboard and recover them. The divers were very skilled, and never seemed to fail to retrieve the coin, though there must be easier ways to make a living.

At Freetown we saw another contrasting aspect of African life in the arrival of the deck class passengers. They were mostly traders in family groups who lived, ate, slept, and did everything else on a section of the foredeck that was out of bounds to other passengers, though clearly visible from the deck above. There was no privacy, and apparently no sanitation in this area, and certainly no temptation to other passengers to trespass. When the wind was in the wrong direction, it was not exactly fragrant.

The luxurious food on board had seemed less and less attractive as time went by. It was not that the quality of the food deteriorated, but rather that our appetites diminished with the warmer weather and the limited opportunities to burn up energy with physical activity. Glenys' appetite lasted longer than mine, but eventually she too succumbed and one evening we both skipped dinner and retired early. Helen, who had had her own stomach problems a few days earlier, saw that Glenys was off colour, and very sympathetically offered Mummy her beloved Teddy for comfort.

In a couple more days we arrived at our immediate destination, Tema, the port for Accra, the capital of Ghana. Here we were to break our journey in order to teach at an introductory course in linguistics held on the premises of the University of Ghana at Legon on the outskirts of Accra. For the period of our absence from England, we had been granted short-term membership of the Summer

Institute of Linguistics (SIL). We had already had close contact with SIL in England for several years, and had been both students and teachers on their linguistics courses there. So in return for the administrative and logistical support of SIL for our time in Nigeria, we were contributing six weeks to help with the course they were running in Ghana.

We were met by Cyril, a local SIL representative, who was allowed to come on board to bring us our entry permits for immigration before we disembarked. The cabins contained fruit bowls, and in our cabin the bowl still held a couple of apples. These to our surprise Cyril was only too eager to polish off. We had not realised that apples do not grow in West Africa, and that for him they were a rare luxury. It was to be over a year before we had a good supply of apples again.

Going through customs was a fairly slow business with long queues, but not particularly troublesome. When our turn came and we were talking to the customs officer, Helen, safely ensconced in her pushchair, dropped her Teddy, and the customs man bent down and picked it up for her. Four years earlier I had spent one week as part of an SIL course studying Gã, the main language spoken in the Accra area. Suddenly and providentially the long forgotten Gã phrase for "Thank you" popped unbidden into my mind, and I was able to come out with it. I'm not sure who was more surprised, the customs man or me, but a big smile spread across his face, and our customs clearance was soon over. This was an unexpected object lesson to us in the importance of even minimal local language knowledge in establishing relationships. It was also an encouragement to us for what we hoped to achieve in due course in Nigeria. After this high spot came a lower one. Before we left the docks a policeman tried to buy foreign currency from us at black market rates. Whether this was a sting we did not know, but the man accepted our refusal and was not persistent, so we left unhindered.

In 1965, the Elder Dempster passenger ships to West Africa left Liverpool once a fortnight. Within two or three years the frequency dropped to once every six weeks, and within a few more years the voyages were discontinued. The spread of jet aircraft meant that people no longer used ships for business travel, only for holiday cruises. We did not realise it at the time, but our voyage had enabled us to sample the end of an era in long distance travel.

Chapter 2
Prelude in Ghana

Accra, being relatively flat and relatively large, created a very different impression from Freetown. Cyril soon bore us away from the docks to the SIL group house in the suburbs. At least Cyril said it was in the suburbs, though it seemed more like the countryside to us after living in London for several years. The building was quite large and was able to accommodate both resident and transiting members of SIL as well as various people who were there in connection with the linguistics course. We were given two connecting rooms, which meant that Helen could sleep in a separate room, to our mutual satisfaction. The level of humidity was quite comfortable, and the weather was not unduly hot, remaining pleasantly in the 70s and 80s Fahrenheit throughout our stay. Yes, temperatures were all measured in Fahrenheit in those days: for those too young to remember, this is the 20s Celsius.

Right from day one, we found the flora and fauna fascinating. Our first surprise was the deafening chorus after dark. Prominent among the singers were frogs and crickets, but no doubt there were plenty of other contributors that we never identified. One performer on the first evening was so loud and shrill and insistent that I thought it was a kettle whistling, and wondered why nobody turned it off. The frogs would come onto the verandah, and Helen's exercise after tea was to chase them in the hope of catching one. One evening she actually succeeded, and it was hard to tell whether Helen or the frog was more taken aback. He suffered no harm from his misadventure, however, and she enjoyed the pleasant flush of unexpected achievement.

Perhaps our most regular source of entertainment came from lizards, creatures that seem to lead pretty secretive lives in England, but are much more extrovert in the tropics. There were several varieties, both indoor and outdoor. Indoors there were plenty of little geckos, light brown in colour and only three or four inches long. Their favourite activity was running across the walls or upside down on the ceiling, and snapping up any mosquitoes or other delicacies that came within reach of their agile tongues. Geckos are completely harmless, and indeed their contribution to keeping down the mosquitoes was more than welcome. Occasionally one would lose its grip on the ceiling and land with a plop on the floor (or the table!), but they always seemed to scuttle away with no harm done. Most geckos had tails, but they also had the ability to shed their tails in time of danger, and now and then we noticed one whose tail was shorter than the others, though what their predators were we never saw.

Outside in the yard there were other much bigger lizards. One kind had black and white stripes down their backs, and bright blue tails. The largest, called agama lizards, could be well over a foot long, and the males were very colourful, with red at their heads, changing to orange to yellow to brown along the length of their backs. They liked to bask in the sun on the tops of walls, often doing press-ups, though whether this was simply exercise, or perhaps some kind of territorial behaviour we did not know.

Butterflies and moths were another source of wonder, both in size and in colour, though because of the erratic nature of their movements, they were much more difficult to observe with any precision. Moths of course were drawn towards any source of light in the evenings, and self-incinerated moths could be found under any light-bulb. One quickly learnt not to sit directly under a light with an evening drink.

Other indoor inhabitants that we were unused to included ants, not the kind of ants common in gardens in England, but tiny little ants that marched in orderly columns to and from anywhere that something sweet had been spilt. It was quite impossible to get rid of them, so there was a state of peaceful co-existence with them. They did no harm to us, so we did no harm to them, at least not deliberately, though they must have been inadvertently trodden on occasionally. But we tried not to spill sweet things, or if we did, to mop them up quickly. There were crickets of various musical abilities around, but the most interesting representative of the grasshopper family was the praying mantis, an insect a couple of inches long that always stood with its hands folded devoutly in front, giving rise to its name.

The creatures that really caught Helen's imagination were the spiders. We had never seen such large specimens, or indeed such mutilated ones. Like the geckos, they tended to keep to the ceilings, but many of them appeared to be war veterans, some with only seven legs, some with six, and one with only five. Whether these amputees had survived gecko strikes or some other kind of attack we never had the chance to observe, but they were a regular source of horrid fascination, especially it seemed in the bathroom where they would glare balefully at you from above the shower. The shower itself was unpredictable. If there was a power cut, the water also stopped for some arcane reason, and if you were already covered in soap, this was not very convenient, as power cuts could last for some time. So the first thing to do when showering was to fill an emergency bucket with water just in case the main supply died on you.

Helen was just beginning to talk, and our records of her speech development associated with the short period that we were in Ghana enable us to be pretty accurate in dating them. Her rendering of "spider" was "seesee," but the range of meaning of this term included flies, frogs, lizards, or anything else not big enough to be considered a "dodu." This word was derived from "dog", but its range of meaning included sheep, goats, any other quadruped, and at first even hens. Eventually a third zoological category emerged, namely "birbie." This was her rendering of "bird", and covered not only hens, but crows, kites, vultures and anything else with feathers and wings. These are all terms for classes of items, but soon one particular item emerged with its own special name, "Dedi" for her precious Teddy. Thus far, all her vocabulary was taken from English because that was the language everyone in the group house used. There were of course Ghanaian languages spoken in the area around, but she was not in sufficiently regular contact with their speakers to pick up any words.

Helen's experiments also caused a certain amount of consternation and hilarity in the kitchen. On one occasion someone boiled a kettle of water and was disconcerted to find the contents coming out bright green - thanks to a flower thoughtfully placed inside the kettle. On another occasion the water came out black, and the culprits were two dominoes with their spots boiled off. Well, if empty kettles are left within reach of a toddler...

Another area of life that brought us plenty of new experiences was eating. Some staple items like potatoes were missing, but we had plenty of plantains, large savoury bananas which could be cut into thin slices and fried, coming out rather like chips. Other delicacies included pumpkin, okra (somewhat like cucumber in appearance, but eaten fried), egg plant (rather like aubergine, but to my perception tastier), very hot green peppers, and avocado pears. Though avocados are readily available in British supermarkets nowadays, this was not so forty years ago, and we had never seen them before. Both then and now, they seem to me overrated, and I have never had much enthusiasm for them. In the fruit line there were plenty of bananas, limes, oranges, and pineapples, but the big discovery for us was pawpaws. Pawpaw and lime became and remains a favourite dessert. Helen would have been happy to live on bananas, and most mealtimes were enlivened by delighted cries of "nanu."

Fresh milk was not available, and all milk was made up from milk powder imported from Holland or Denmark. This remained the situation throughout our time in West Africa, but Helen accepted it quite happily and was none the worse for it. Meat was available but very expensive, though there was a good supply of tasty and nutritious fish. Eggs were not easy to come by, and were quite dear, and goods like butter and even margarine were both scarce and very expensive. Ghana was at that time in what proved to be the final year of the Nkrumah regime, and was not far off bankruptcy, so imported goods were real luxuries when they could be found at all. We even heard of "margarine riots," and when new batches of margarine became available in the shops, they were gone in no time. Because of SIL's association with the university, its members had access to the university buttery, which had some sort of priority on imported goods, and this made the situation a little easier, but not much. We made few expeditions into town to the shops, partly because there was so little to buy. The Kingsway department store contained row upon row of empty shelves, and we wondered how it managed to maintain enough turnover to keep open at all.

Fruit, vegetables and fish could all be bought in local markets, and the preparation and clearing up of food at the group house was mostly done by a couple of Ghanaian fellows employed for this purpose. Given the difficult economic situation, they and Nancy, the group house hostess, did a very creditable job. Nobody left the meal table hungry. The foreigners staying in the group house came from a variety of countries, and we were gradually introduced to food customs and preferences that we had not met before. The star turn came one day from John, an American participant in the linguistics course, who put marmalade on kippers. We were relieved to find that even the other Americans considered this mixture idiosyncratic. But is it so very different from putting apple sauce on pork, or redcurrant jelly on turkey?

The course we had come to teach on was held on the university premises at Legon, about eight miles from the group house. Lessons took place in the mornings and the late afternoons, with a break for lunch and a siesta. One of us would teach in the morning and the other in the afternoon, so that someone was always available to keep an eye on Helen. We travelled to and fro in various vehicles, and one day the front axle of the car I was in broke, bringing us to an abrupt halt. Unusually there were two vehicles in use on this occasion, so we were able to be ferried to the university in the other vehicle. And providentially the breakdown took place outside the house of someone known to the driver, so that it was quickly possible to telephone and make arrangements for the car to be towed away and repaired.

There were nine students, two Ghanaians and seven expatriates, all faced with language learning needs of one kind or another. There were three main strands to the course, phonetics, phonemics, and grammar. Phonetics was mainly my responsibility, and phonemics was mainly Glenys', though we were both able to swap roles at need. Phonetics introduces a wide range of the sounds that the human vocal tract can produce, and phonemics deals with the way a selection of these sounds operates systematically within any specific language. An understanding of this is particularly important in formulating alphabets for previously unwritten languages, of which there were a good number in Ghana at that time. The third strand, grammar, was mainly the responsibility of Elaine, an English SIL member normally working in Nigeria who had come to Ghana to teach on the course. It deals with the way words are formed and combined into sentences to convey meaning. Learning any language as an adult requires some understanding of all three topics, but this is especially vital if the language has not been written down before.

The classrooms were in a single storey wooden building looking out onto a square somewhat reminiscent of an Oxbridge college court, though the vegetation was of course very different as well as the architecture. The central grass area was surrounded by an attractive hedge of bushes that looked rather like privets, but whose leaves gradually turned from green to white and then to pink. The journeys to and from the university brought various other sights and sounds to our attention. Huge anthills were found from time to time beside the road. The highest we saw was about twelve feet high, though of course when it rained, they were eroded a little. We often passed sheep and goats, which were surprisingly difficult to distinguish for people fresh from Europe. Both animals were about the same size and the sheep lacked the woolly fleece we would expect. We eventually learnt that if their ears stuck up they were probably goats and if their ears hung down, they were probably sheep. But our difficulty shed a new light on the parable of Jesus in Matthew 25 where the shepherd has to sort out sheep from goats.

On the cultural side, we became accustomed to seeing women walking along with loads carried on their heads, and very often a baby tied up in a cloth on their backs. We also got used to the so-called "Mammy wagons," lorries used as public transport with the back occupied by passengers, especially women with goods to sell in the market. These lorries usually carried intriguing slogans painted on the front or sides or both. These varied from the highly practical such as "Pay the boy now," or "Mind your own," to the more spiritual, such as "Give all to God." In the light of the way some of them were driven, perhaps the most insightful was "Future is unknown."

Our friend from the ship, Mrs. Haylock, was staying in Accra with some English friends, a Mr. and Mrs. Scott, and we were invited to their home a couple of times. The Scotts had been living for eight years in Ghana, where Mr. Scott worked for the Ghana Broadcasting Corporation. They lived in a bungalow with a garden in which were growing some red peppers. Mr. Scott gave me a few and I was naive enough and rash enough to put one in my mouth. I quickly learnt to treat red peppers with great respect.

There were also opportunities to make a few short trips out of Accra at weekends. The first was to the Volta River dam at Akosombo, about 60 miles from the city. We travelled in a convoy of three vehicles to the gorge where the dam was under construction. One of the students on the course knew an engineer working at the site, and so we were given a guided tour and allowed to drive right across the top of the dam, which offered splendid views of the river both above and below the dam itself. At that stage of course the water level had not reached the final planned level. The project was intended not only to provide a regular water supply but also to be a source of hydroelectric power. In this respect it was a significant symbol of development in post-colonial Africa. However, the building of the dam would eventually inundate about ten per cent of the land area of Ghana, and drive many people out of their traditional villages, so it was by no means an unmitigated blessing to all Ghanaians.

A second trip took us to Winneba, about 40 miles west of Accra on the coast. There we were the weekend guests of a young English couple called Colin and Gill who had been members of the same church we had attended in London when we were first married. They were now lecturing in a Teacher's Training College at Winneba, and thoroughly enjoying themselves there. We were able to bathe in the sea, an experience that Helen found really exhilarating. The waves were quite big, and the water surprisingly cold so near the equator, but she was not a whit intimidated, and did not want to come out of the water. On that beach we also made the acquaintance of ghost crabs, tiny little creatures that are almost transparent and scuttle about at high speed. When we visited the market, we were amazed to find large numbers of vultures walking around hopefully among the shoppers. Though they look rather sinister and threatening with their featherless heads and sharp beaks, they were not aggressive, and were simply ignored by the people. Nevertheless they were almost as big as Helen, so we picked her up and carried her while they were around.

Like us, Colin was a Bristolian. On the Sunday morning we managed to pick up a church service from England on the BBC, and were pleasantly surprised to find that the speaker was also from Bristol, and well known to us. In fact I had been in his Bible Class as a teenager. This was a very happy reminder of home that somehow put the icing on the cake of a very relaxing weekend.

Our last excursion was a shorter one, to the botanical garden at Aburi in the Akwapim hills about 25 miles from Accra. It was the season when there was more fruit than flowers, and we saw such exotic items as cinnamon, nutmeg, cocoa, guavas, and cola nuts. Flowers had been somewhat frustrating to us in Ghana. We had appreciated their beauty, but were unable to name them. The expatriates usually did not know the English name, and the Ghanaians were not very interested: if they were not edible, why bother with them? We had little spare time and lacked the resources to pursue the question, so reluctantly had to remain ignorant. Almost the only flowers we were able to pin a label on were on a so-called flamboyant tree. Not surprisingly, they were bright red.

Our time in Ghana was drawing to a close, and a very smooth and gentle introduction to Africa it had given us. The teaching came to an end, exams were set and marked, and we had to repack our cases and think about the next stage of our travels. Helen knew that something was afoot to disrupt the routine she had become used to, but could not understand what it was. Eventually Cyril took us and our baggage back to Tema and we embarked again on the MV Accra for the short journey on to Lagos in Nigeria. Helen's belongings included four more teeth than she had arrived with. The cabin we were allotted this time was not as good as the one we had had before. The cold water tap ran hot, the hot tap ran almost boiling, and there was inadequate space for Helen's cot in the cabin. But it was only for one night – our third wedding anniversary.

Chapter 3
To the Ekpeye

Arriving in Nigeria was a much less pleasant experience than arriving in Ghana. There were far more passengers disembarking from the ship in Apapa, the port of Lagos, so the queues for immigration and customs were a lot longer. In fact Glenys and I had to take turns to have breakfast in order to keep a place in the queue. When we finally reached the customs, we were in for a nasty shock. The Central Research Fund of London University had provided a new tape recorder for use in the language research that was the main purpose of our time in Africa, and although it did not belong to us, we had to pay 100% duty on it, £60. There were trivial duties on other items, making a total of £72. Although that does not sound much today, it was a lot in 1965, especially for impecunious students, and I had to cash all our travellers' cheques in order to pay it. So our exchequer was seriously depleted before we even left the docks.

But the worst moment came when all our baggage was cleared and we were free to leave. This involved going down in a large lift, the kind where you go in at one end and out at the other. We put Helen, asleep in her pushchair, at the front end, then all the baggage, with ourselves at the back. When the lift door opened at the lower floor, we were totally unprepared for the waiting horde of porters, all yelling at the tops of their voices. Naturally, they woke Helen up and she started to cry, but we could not get to her easily because of all the baggage between her and us. Eventually I struggled past it, but it was a hard task to fend off all but a few of the porters, keep an eye on the various bits of baggage and reassure Helen all at once. The sudden pandemonium was enough to stretch our nerves to breaking point, and by the time I had regained some measure of control, Glenys was in tears as well as Helen.

Fortunately the transportation firm we had booked to take the bulk of our goods from Lagos to Enugu in what was then called the Eastern Region of Nigeria had turned up with a van, and once the porters had calmed down, they did an amazing job of getting our stuff into the van. One man carried a box containing a kerosene-operated fridge on top of his head, and another did the same with a 45-gallon oil drum that we had used as a waterproof container. They each had help from others in getting the load up onto their heads, but carrying the load was still an awe-inspiring achievement even though the distance was not very great. They certainly earned the "dashes" (tips) that they received.

When the van had relieved us of our heavy goods we were able to take a taxi to a mission guest house where we were to spend a couple of nights. We certainly felt in need of a rest! Although it was 2.30 p.m. by the time we arrived, they had kept some lunch for us, and we were more than grateful for this kindness. The next day Elaine, with whom we had shared the teaching in Ghana, arrived by air, and we all got ready for the land journey to Enugu the following day. This too turned out to be a very stressful day. In Nigeria the way to travel was by inter-city taxi, normally a Peugeot 404 estate car with three rows of seats, holding seven passengers. There were no safety belts! With three adults, a toddler and a lot of luggage, we planned to take a whole taxi and have a journey that was not too squashed. We got up early and I set off for the lorry park. Not having any idea where it was, I was at the mercy of taxi drivers who tried to take me elsewhere, and I ended up back at the guest house with no Peugeot.

Elaine was more experienced and knowledgeable, so after breakfast we all went together to the lorry park. Most of the taxis going our way had already left, but after a lot of wrangling and haggling, we finally obtained a taxi, and returned to the guest house to collect our belongings before setting off eastwards. At that time the bridge over the River Niger had not yet been completed, so this taxi could take us only the 285 miles to Asaba on the west

bank of the river. There we would have to cross the river
on a ferry and find another taxi to go on the remaining 66
miles to Enugu. The road from Lagos to Asaba had one
lane in each direction, but once we had left the city behind
the traffic was not heavy. The road was surfaced for much
of the way, but from time to time deteriorated into a mass
of deeply rutted mud, and the situation was not helped by
the rain that accompanied us most of the way.

The only town of any size along the road was Benin,
and apart from that, the route was almost entirely
through rain forest so the scenery was monotonous and
not particularly interesting. The land was punctuated by
frequent small rivers running through shallow valleys,
and these were the really scary places. The road would
invariably swoop down to the river, cross the bridge, and
then ascend again the other side. The problem was that
the bridges were usually single track, so if another vehicle
was approaching the bridge from the opposite direction
at the same time, the drivers liked to play chicken, and
instead of slowing down for the bridges, they actually
accelerated. Not surprisingly, there were wrecked vehicles
here and there along the road. The driver we had engaged
in Lagos turned out to be a wild man, and our hearts were
in our mouths every time we came to a river. At one place
he did force another driver off the road, but by the grace
of God we eventually arrived at Asaba safely. Helen

was completely unruffled by the journey, and indeed was unbelievably good the whole way.

I had naively assumed that the driver would have some basic English, and in all probability he himself was under the same impression. However, our perceptions of what constituted basic English and his did not overlap much, and this gave us our first taste of West African pidgin. At one point I tried to engage the driver in conversation, and asked what I thought was a simple question, "Where is your home town?" After a couple of repetitions, he had evidently not understood the question, and I had not understood whatever response he had made. Elaine came to my rescue by putting the question in pidgin as "Fo what place yo modda de born yo?" This he understood perfectly. I no longer remember his answer, but I had at least learnt enough not to try any further small talk!

When we reached Asaba the rain had stopped, so we were able to get across the river on the ferry without much problem, but we then had to find transport onward from Onitsha to Enugu. It was getting dark, there were no Peugeots to be had, and we were very low on money. To complicate the situation, the heavens opened and with nowhere convenient to shelter, we were all quickly soaked to the skin. We put the cover on Helen's pushchair to give her what protection we could, but she was delighted with the downpour and leaned out as far as she could in order to get as wet as possible. After half an hour or so we managed to find a Morris Minor that was willing to make the trip to Enugu, and squeezed ourselves and our luggage into it. Before we had even left the town, the driver, an older and less reckless man than the previous one, decided that one of his tyres was not reliable enough for an inter-city journey, so he spent a while driving round town until he could find a different vehicle for us. When he succeeded, it was only another Morris Minor, and we then had to transfer all our luggage to the other vehicle, still in heavy rain. Once we were finally on our way I took off my sodden shirt, and travelled topless, but the ladies preferred to retain their dignity and their wet blouses.

We received a warm welcome at the SIL group house in Enugu, where we immediately had to borrow money to pay the taxi driver. We were relieved to find that our camera and especially the tape recorder had escaped any damage from the rain. We did not know it at the time, but our worst experiences in Nigeria were now behind us.

SIL had invitations from numerous language areas to send teams to do linguistic analysis and develop scripts for hitherto unwritten languages, but the number of invitations exceeded the number of available staff. Our arrival meant that work could be started in one more language, and Ekpeye was the one selected for us. Our hope was to go to our assigned language area as soon as possible, but of course we could not leave Enugu until our goods had arrived from Lagos and we had had the opportunity to buy six months' worth of supplies of things that would not be available in a remote village. The difficulty was that we could not be sure what would be available, so had to do some of our shopping by guesswork. The shops in Enugu, unlike those in Accra, were well stocked, and somewhat to our surprise the two with the best range of supplies (Chellaram's and Chanrai's) were both owned and run by Indian traders. We patronised them both for different items, and by buying in bulk were able to get wholesale prices. So we soon found ourselves the unaccustomed owners of 50 lbs of flour, 60 lbs of sugar, 30 tins of powdered milk, 20 lbs of rice, 24 large packets of Corn Flakes, 36 lbs of margarine, 30 packet soups, and a few dozen tins of different sorts of meat and processed cheese, as well as smaller quantities of a variety of other items. Perhaps our prize acquisition was a foam rubber double mattress to go over the two camp beds that we had in our freight for sleeping on in the village. This we acquired not from the luxury of a shop, but by bargaining in the market for a lower price than the shops could offer. It cost us the princely sum of ten guineas and was not just for comfort, but also had the very practical purpose of giving us something to tuck our mosquito nets under.

There were a few practical skills that we gained a little experience of before going to the village. Glenys had a few tries at baking bread, and we also practised cutting each other's hair. I viewed the prospect of having my hair cut by an amateur with greater equanimity than she did, though I was convinced that my skills in this field were not a whit inferior to hers. When we eventually returned to England and she went to a hairdresser again, she explained apologetically that her hair had been cut by her husband for the past year. The hairdresser examined it critically and to Glenys' astonishment and my delight announced that she had seen it done worse professionally.

Most days we went for a walk with Helen, and of course a fair-haired child attracted a good deal of attention from the Nigerian children, who would follow us with cries in Igbo of *"Ony'acha, ony'acha"* (white man, white man). They loved to touch Helen's arms and hair, and she never seemed to mind. But the big draw was her pushchair. A few of the bolder children would ask permission to push it, which we let them do under close supervision as long as they did it gently. Those who did very obviously gained status among their peers! Their standard all-purpose greeting was "Byebye," which Helen quickly picked up.

After about ten days in Enugu we were ready to set off again, and all our goods and chattels were loaded onto a VW minibus belonging to SIL. We had had our doubts about whether they would all fit in, but they did. Nigeria drove on the left, but the minibus was a left hand drive vehicle, so one was driving on the wrong side, though this did not prove to be a serious handicap. We were accompanied by Werner, a Swiss member of the SIL

35

team, who would bring the minibus back to Enugu. Our immediate destination was a town called Ahoada, situated at the eastern edge of the Niger Delta. It was the main centre of the area where the Ekpeye language was spoken, and was also the place where the Southern Baptist mission had a house, though the resident missionary was on leave at that time. We had been given permission to use the house for a night or two until we could find somewhere more permanent.

The 160-mile journey south passed uneventfully, and near the market in Ahoada we stopped to ask where the Baptist house was. A crowd materialised at once, and a local lad of about 15 held his arms out to Helen. To our surprise she took to him instantly, held her arms out and went to him without hesitation. We learnt that his name was Bob. Once we had found the right house, we were made welcome by the local Baptist minister, Rev. Howard Ikiriko. We unloaded the minibus, then while Glenys unpacked the basic necessities, Werner and I went a further 18 miles on an unsealed road to an area where the Abuan language was spoken. There we made a brief visit to another SIL family from England, Ian and Amelia. Though we had met them before, we did not know them well, but during our year in Nigeria they became and still remain firm friends. At our request, they had had a wooden cot made for Helen and this we took back to Ahoada for her to use.

When we got back to Ahoada, Glenys was frustrated that she had not made as much progress as she would have liked with preparing food, but in the absence of electricity, we soon got the kerosene lamps going and managed to eat. For company we had Herb, a Canadian member of another mission who was travelling in the area, and trying to develop interest in literature distribution.

Next day Werner nobly looked after the preparation of food, leaving Glenys and me free to go around in the minibus looking for accommodation under the guidance of Rev. Ikiriko. We looked at several places in Ahoada itself, but they were all either too noisy, too expensive, or in areas where Igbo rather than Ekpeye was the language spoken by neighbours. So in the end we decided on a house in a sizeable village called Orupata, a couple of miles outside Ahoada. The language spoken around us there would be almost 100% Ekpeye. Moreover Orupata was situated on the only sealed road in the area, and so was of easier access than most other villages. The road went about 16 miles to Mbiama on the Orashi River, and from there it was a ride upriver on a launch to Joinkrama, where Elaine and her American colleague Joy were working on the Engenni language, and where the Southern Baptists had a hospital with several mission staff. We would thus be about midway between Elaine and Joy in one direction, and Ian and Amelia in the other, which could prove convenient for all of us.

The name of our village regularly appeared in written form as Orupata, though when we got to know the Ekpeye sound system, we realised that this spelling did not correspond very well with the Ekpeye pronunciation. We never discovered the source of what seemed to be the official spelling. Perhaps it represented some sort of assimilation to Igbo pronunciation, or perhaps it went back to colonial days and was nothing more than a mishearing on the part of a British administrator. A more accurate spelling would have been Ulupata, but we always used the official form in our letters home, and will continue to do so in this account.

The building we rented was being built by an Ekpeye man who was working in Lagos and investing his earnings in his home village. His brother Elijah was acting on his behalf as the landlord. The house was made of concrete blocks with a roof of corrugated zinc (locally called pan), and had no less than seven rooms and a verandah. The rent asked was the princely sum of five pounds per month. Probably the rent was so low because nobody really expected foreigners to go and live in a bush village.

We had been introduced to the landlord by the local councillor, Mr. Ebeku, an acquaintance of Rev. Ikiriko. Now renting a house is a serious business, especially in a village where such things do not happen every day, and it was felt that a contract should be drawn up to solemnise the occasion. Since nobody else wanted to do the actual writing, this job was left to me. When I presented everyone involved with a contract that was properly typed with carbon copies, it was felt that the deal was prestigious indeed. I signed my name, Elijah, who was not literate, added his thumb-print, and Mr. Ebeku acted as witness. Happily the contract was respected by everyone involved, and we never had any problems arising from it. So the following morning we moved in, and now that we were, in a manner of speaking, settled, Werner left us on our own, taking the minibus back to Enugu.

The house windows had wooden shutters with bolts on the inside, and doors at back and front that both locked and bolted. At the back was quite a large walled garden containing a lot of sugar cane and a few canna lilies, with four mysterious little rooms abutting the far wall. These, we were told, were kitchens – one for each wife! (For better or worse I never had the opportunity to test how well they would get on with each other.) Cooking in the village was done on wood fires in the open, so in this house the kitchens were some distance from the main building both to keep the smoke away and to reduce the fire risk. The house itself was completely bare, with a cement floor and not even a ceiling to protect us from the heat radiated by the metal roof.

There were one or two jobs that needed doing before we could be really comfortable in our new home, the main one being the digging of a latrine. This was organised by Elijah in the space behind the far wall of the garden, and provided entertainment for the whole village. None of the villagers needed a latrine – what else was the surrounding jungle there for? The project was carried out under the supervision of the local handyman, one Nathan, a competent little fellow with a notable limp, perhaps the result of polio in childhood. First a hole several feet deep was dug. This was not too difficult a task as the whole Niger Delta area was composed of alluvial sand. The water table was not very far below the surface at that time of year. Then a small square hut was built over the hole, with a wooden frame, mud walls and a palm thatch roof, a miniature version of the majority of the houses in the village. There was hardly room to stand up inside the hut, but then one didn't really go in there to stand up. There was a little wood and thatch door that could be pulled across the entrance to provide the privacy that Europeans inexplicably considered necessary. And to cap it all, there was even a wooden fence put around the whole structure. We had no say at all in the design and construction of the latrine, our lot being merely to bankroll it. The total cost came to four pounds ten shillings, so we didn't feel that we had a bad bargain. And with nothing to break down, the latrine served its purpose effortlessly throughout our stay.

The other major construction job was setting up two poles in concrete bases so that Glenys could have a clothes line. Nathan was called in again, and the project was explained to him. No doubt this seemed even more outlandish to him than the latrine, but he realised that there was an honest penny to be turned, and he was happy to turn it. Once he understood what we wanted, he murmured "Make I go bush get stick" and the project was under way. We did wonder whether a "stick" would be strong enough to support the weight of wet clothes, but on his return it became clear that this was pidgin for timber. Nathan set up two sturdy poles in strong concrete bases and the clothes line never gave us any trouble. Total cost for materials and labour, one pound eighteen shillings and six pence.

Apart from our camp beds and mattress and Helen's cot, we had a couple of folding chairs, the kerosene fridge, and a kerosene cooker with two burners that Elaine had lent us. We gradually acquired a table and several wooden chairs from Patrick, the local carpenter. As we unpacked, the packing cases were transformed into cupboards, and I added some hardboard shelves to the inside of the box the fridge had been transported in. My ineptitude at such tasks was matched only by Patrick's inability to control his mirth on seeing the results of my efforts. We also had a plastic baby bath for Helen, and soon discovered that in the absence of any other facility, we could just about fit into it, and take turns to pour water over each other. On a concrete floor spillage did not matter.

The water supply was a well just outside the hedge at the front of the house. It was just a hole in the ground with a log across the top to stand on, but no protection around it at all. And as we found out in the dry season, it was the best well in the village, still producing water when other wells had dried up. The water became very muddy in the dry season, but it was still water, and we had two large urns to boil it in, and filters to make it if not clear, at least less opaque. The further the dry season advanced, the more often the porous filter candles had to be taken out of the filter and scrubbed, but it was a task worth doing to get clearer drinking water.

It was Glenys' constant dread that Helen might fall into the well, but happily she never took any interest in it. She was much more interested in a pile of periwinkle shells in the front yard. Their presence was a bit of a mystery to us, but we discovered that when cement was made, they would be crushed up and put into the mixture to strengthen it. Presumably they were intended for use whenever any further building took place in the house. Helen soon learnt the Ekpeye word for a periwinkle shell (*echechela*, which she simplified to *chilala*) and is probably to this day the only European child who has ever been in possession of this particular nugget of information.

During the wet season, especially at the peak of the monsoon from July to September, there was another source of water, rain. Our house was shaped like the lower half of the letter H, so there were two gutters channelling rain water from the roof in a powerful jet into the back garden. We acquired an old oil drum and placed it strategically to catch the rain. If there was time to do so, it paid to move it when the rain first began, because the first run-off water brought with it a lot of dust and other odds and ends from the roof. But once the rain was pouring down, it did not take much time to fill the drum and so collect 45 gallons of water that was very useful for things like washing clothes. If it rained hard in the evening, we would sometimes go and stand under it ourselves and so enjoy a brisk and surprisingly cold shower. Glenys found a heavy shower a good time to wash her hair and give it a very thorough rinse.

One room of the house was occupied entirely by agama lizards, dozens of them, many of them monsters well over a foot long. They did not seem to be aware of the conditions of our contract as sole tenants, and as they were harmless and that room had no window so that we could hardly use it for any other purpose, we decided that we would just keep our oil drums and tinned food in there. So we tolerated our uninvited sub-tenants in a sort of unarmed but wary neutrality. They made no attempt to encroach on our territory, so we left them in peace to enjoy theirs. Where they came from and what they fed on we never discovered. There were also plenty of little geckos running around the walls in the rest of the house, but we were accustomed to them by now, and indeed rather enjoyed them, not least for their efforts to keep the mosquitoes down.

At last we could begin the main task that had brought us to Africa!

Chapter 4
Settling In

How would you go about learning an unwritten language? We had had some practical training from SIL, and I had had some rather theoretical instruction at SOAS, but living for the first time among real people who speak a language you do not understand is a challenge for which nothing can fully prepare you. Even at the beginning of our time in Orupata we were not completely cut off from communication because quite a lot of people, mainly men, had acquired some English either at school or at various jobs they had been able to get from time to time. This "English" was often heavily pidginised, so that we had to adapt our processes of understanding. It was much harder to adapt our speech patterns, and because our aim was to communicate in Ekpeye, we did not make much effort to speak pidgin. Of course Glenys and I spoke to each other in what we considered normal English, but we were more than once asked by people who thought they understood English what language we were speaking. When we insisted that we were speaking English, the admiring response was, "Ah, you people speak fo latingramma."

"Latin grammar" was apparently the pidgin for English as spoken by the English, in contrast with the pidginised English spoken along the West Coast of Africa, and known as "wescos."

To begin learning Ekpeye we needed two things. One was regular sessions with people who knew both Ekpeye and English, and the other was conversation with people who knew only Ekpeye. The first could be prepared for and guided in directions we wanted to go in. The second was completely unpredictable and uncontrolled, and could be in turns embarrassing, frustrating, entertaining, hilarious and sometimes even encouraging and satisfying. For regular sessions we were very fortunate to have the help of several good people who came to spend time with us regularly.

First was Rev. Howard Ikiriko, the Baptist minister who had already helped us so much with practical matters. He not only had competent English, but had also given some thought to the structure of his own language. He had tried to translate the Gospel of Mark into Ekpeye, and therefore also had a ready grasp of the problems of putting the language into writing. This meant that he was able not merely to supply us with actual language data, but also to understand the kind of problems we faced in trying to analyse the data and to recognise the basic structures of the language. Such a person is an invaluable asset to anyone attempting to learn a language from scratch with no grammar or dictionary, and we were very grateful for his regular and perceptive help. This extended also to practical matters. It was not difficult for Glenys to buy an ankle length wrap-around cloth in the market so that she could be dressed more like the local women. However for me to acquire the loose suit of light cloth that was "smart casual" for men, and that Rev. Ikiriko often wore, required the services of a tailor. And that made the assistance of a culture broker desirable to help me deal appropriately with the tailor, which included bargaining for a reasonable price. Rev. Ikiriko guided me through this procedure, and I was often glad of the light clothing in the hot climate. The cloth I chose was striped and did make the suit look rather like pyjamas when it was stitched up. After many years in a trunk, it was recently resurrected, and now on warm nights, it does duty as real pyjamas.

After a couple of weeks Rev. Ikiriko announced casually that his wife had delivered "a male child" the previous night. It was their fifth child, and apparently brought little disruption to their lives! As the only ordained Ekpeye minister in any of the local churches, he was a person of some prestige, so his involvement in our instruction lent the project a certain respectability. Because he was the only ordained minister, he was the only Ekpeye man with the title "Reverend," and we soon learnt that everybody treated this as if it were a personal name rather than a title. Before long we also conformed, and that became our normal way of referring to him.

We needed more than one regular helper, however, and since such help was paid for, there was no shortage of applicants. Several of them introduced themselves by means of a letter written in English, or what the writer imagined to be English. We regret that we did not keep some of them, but one we remember clearly. It came from a young man who introduced himself by the name that sounded to us like Mettu Sallay. It didn't seem a very plausible name, but when we read his letter and saw the signature, we realised that his name was actually Methuselah. He must have been at least fifteen!

One of the applicants was Bob, the lad in the market to whom Helen had gone so willingly. He seemed an intelligent and responsible young man, so we decided to back Helen's instinct, and hired him. He turned out to be a good choice, and we never regretted our decision. He lived not in Orupata, but in another village called Ekpena, about a mile beyond Ahoada on the opposite bank of the Sambreiro River. This meant he had a journey of about three miles each way to visit us, which was often made on foot. This did not bother him at all, and it gave him the distinction of being employed, a privilege shared by few young fellows of his age. The wage of one shilling an hour (five pence in decimal currency) may not sound much, but it was quite acceptable by local standards. Though Bob had had only six years of primary education, he took a real interest in our work, and showed a quick grasp of the problems we faced. In later months when we were recording stories on our tape recorder, he proved to be a very reliable transcriber of the spoken word onto paper.

Bob and Helen became firm friends, and when his work with us was over, he would often stay in Orupata for a while and take Helen around the village in her pushchair, no doubt gaining added kudos thereby. There was of course no Ekpeye word for a pushchair, so the word for bicycle, *igwe*, quickly acquired an extended meaning. If it became necessary to distinguish the pushchair from an ordinary bicycle, that was no problem either – it was the *bebe-igwe*.

The Baptist lay pastor in Orupata, Okpara, also felt some responsibility for our welfare. He was a kindly and well-meaning man about our own age, and helped me to buy a bicycle in Ahoada. This was a more complex operation than it may sound. First of all nobody would believe that a European wanted to go around on a bicycle, because everybody knows that Europeans always go around in vehicles. When they finally accepted that I really did want a bicycle, they would not believe that a European would buy anything other than a new bicycle. But persistence eventually reaped its reward, and we acquired a second-hand ladies bicycle on which Glenys and/or I could go in and out of town. There was a cycle mechanic called Morrison who plied his trade in Orupata, so punctures and any other minor repairs could be dealt with conveniently near home.

Bicycles were a common form of transport for a whole family. We had encountered the pidgin expression "enta bicycle," and at first found it a bit mystifying. Entering a bus is one thing, but how do you "enter" a bicycle? We soon found out. Father sits on the seat and provides the pedal power, often with the oldest child sitting on the cross-bar, a smaller one on the handle-bar, and mother sitting side-saddle on the luggage rack at the back, with the latest baby in her arms. Progress even on the surfaced road was usually slow and wobbly, so it was just as well that there was little motor traffic.

Okpara decided to appoint himself our third language helper. However he had little education and never came to understand why we asked certain sorts of language questions and not others. After a few weeks it became clear that our times with him were much less productive than those with Reverend and Bob. We did not want to offend Okpara so we managed to switch him to working in the compound that surrounded our house. Since he still got paid, he didn't seem to mind the change. By the time this happened, we were getting as much information from other people as we could cope with, and did not need a third daily session.

Okpara quickly combined his gardening and pastoral responsibilities towards us by expressing his concern about a gap in the hedge that grew part of the way round our front yard, because it was getting visibly bigger. He was worried that evil spirits might be using it as a way of gaining access to our premises. To our observation, the gap was being enlarged first by the passage of dogs, goats and sheep, and later by children taking a short cut, so we were not unduly bothered. But for some reason that we never got to the bottom of, Okpara's concern increased, and he eventually took matters into his own hands and blocked the gap with sticks. Since this gave him peace of mind (as well as another hour's pay), we raised no objection, though we never understood why any prowling evil spirits could not enter the compound from the side that had no hedge at all!

Unscheduled conversation practice was provided by our neighbours and by casual acquaintances such as other cyclists I met up with on the road to Ahoada. Before many weeks passed I had received requests from fellow travellers to set up a school, a church, a dispensary, and a maternity home. Needless to say, none were fulfilled. The women and children in the village seldom had much English, so we had to use whatever we could of Ekpeye in speaking to them. We soon learnt to negotiate the purchase of the pawpaws, limes, oranges, bananas, pineapples, sweet corn, and coconuts that were regularly offered to us, though our progress in other areas was erratic and distinctly fallible. One of our most common utterances was what we will write here as *"monujiem-m"* – "I don't understand." But people continued to come and chat, and it probably gave them a real boost to realise that there were areas of life where they knew much more than these "educated" foreigners.

Although we often knew the names of the men and the children among our neighbours, we usually did not know the names of the women. They were customarily both addressed and referred to as "wife of X," or if applicable as "mother of Y." This was not in any way derogatory, and we were treated in the same way. I was sometimes addressed as *"ibheke,"* "white man," usually by people who did not know us well. At other times I was *"ida Helen,"* "father of Helen," though this was used more by people who knew us well enough to know Helen's name. In like manner Glenys was sometimes *"ngweny'ibheke,"* "wife of white man," and more often *"ina Helen,"* "mother of Helen." The word *ibheke* was somewhat mystifying to us, as it was a single word, and not at all parallel with the Igbo expression *ony'acha,* that meant literally "white person." One explanation that seemed quite plausible was that it derived from the surname of the first European to explore the area in 1854, Dr. William Balfour Baikie. We knew nothing about him at that time, but many years later while on holiday in the Orkney Islands we came across a memorial to him in St. Magnus' Cathedral, Kirkwall.

Helen was now 18 months old and entering the prime period of language acquisition. Her mastery of English sounds was not yet complete, so her mind was still flexible enough to absorb easily some of the Ekpeye sounds that we found most difficult, and from time to time we were amazed at how well she coped. Ekpeye, like many languages in West Africa, is a tone language, that is to say, a language in which words that sound the same in terms of their consonants and vowels may carry different meanings when the pitch of the syllables changes. Helen absorbed this kind of variation readily, and by the time we left the village, her production of Ekpeye tones was more accurate than ours.

If we were to have maximum time for language study, it would be necessary for us to employ someone to help with routine jobs in the house, and to look after Helen at times when we were working with our language helpers. The idea of having what in earlier times would have been called a servant was rather unpalatable, but from the local point of view, if we failed to do so, this would be perceived as a refusal to share our relative wealth by providing employment for someone who otherwise would have none. This would be seen as evidence of stinginess, and would not tell in our favour. So we had to bite the bullet and become rather hesitant employers.

Choosing the right person could be a tricky task so we sought the advice of Reverend. He recommended a girl of about 18 from his home village of Obholobholo nine miles away, and after a few days she arrived. By this time we had enough furniture to offer her her own room and bed in the house, and she began to settle in. Naturally she had had little or no contact with foreigners before, and was not accustomed to the kind of housekeeping we took for granted. But she had a modest competence in English and seemed willing to learn what Glenys required. It was somewhat hard going for all of us at first but she gradually got used to her duties and we were particularly glad that she got on well with Helen. The complicating factor was that her name was also Helen, but already most people around were calling our Helen "Baby," and she soon came to refer to herself by this name, so there was not too much confusion.

We invited Big Helen to share our meals, but after trying a couple of times, she decided she would prefer to prepare her own, and as there were four kitchens at the end of the garden for her to choose from, this was no problem. One of the things about our food that fascinated our neighbours was the crockery and cutlery that we used to eat it with. This was viewed with a mixture of awe and trepidation. Why not use the fingers God provided you with? Well, that partly depends on what you are eating. Things like corn flakes and milk or tinned stew are not as easy to cope with as slices of boiled yam, or gari, a doughy substance prepared by quite a complicated process from cassava roots.

Although what you eat and how you eat it is at one level a trivial matter, it does illustrate the difficulty of finding a balance in adjustment to an alien culture. We ate quite a lot of local produce especially fruit, but we ate it in a different way. We were there to study the Ekpeye language and live alongside its people, learning about customs and values as well as language. But we were not Ekpeye people, and in the space of one year, had no realistic hope of reaching a deep understanding of their culture. We lacked the social knowledge of how to behave appropriately in different circumstances and with different people. They were intuitively aware of all this, and made allowances for our ineptitude. However, they expected us to behave like Europeans, though their expectations of how Europeans ought to behave did not always match up with either our desires or our finances. This left us making a rather awkward compromise that left nobody fully satisfied. Europeans "ought" to drive around in cars, but all we had was a second hand bicycle. Europeans "ought" to live in a well appointed house with a nice garden, but we were living in what was in effect just the incomplete shell of a house. Well, that was the way things were, and we had to do the best we could to adapt, while recognising that in the available time we could not really succeed.

After the first few hectic days of getting ourselves organised, we settled into something of a routine, though we soon found out that in a village, anything can disrupt a routine at any time. The days began pretty early - when there is no electricity, you don't want to waste the precious hours of daylight. We were only about five degrees north of the equator, so the length of the day did not vary much throughout the year. Even if we had felt like sleeping later, it would hardly have been possible because other people rose at dawn, around six o'clock, and went about their business of lighting fires, fetching water, grating and pounding cassava, and so on, and we could not avoid hearing them. One of the intriguing features of grating the cassava was that when the job was finished, the local goats were allowed to lick the grater clean.

Among the early risers was Big Helen, drawing enough water for us to boil a five-gallon urn that would meet our needs for drinking water for a couple of days. We would have some breakfast, then about 8.30 Reverend would arrive on his bike for our first language session. Baby Helen was still at the stage where she had a sleep right after breakfast, so we usually had no demands from her during the hour-long session. Big Helen would be on the verandah at this time washing clothes, and hanging them on our washing line.

Two or three times a week I would accompany Reverend back into Ahoada to see if there was any mail for us at the Ahoada Post Office. Although Ahoada was hardly a metropolis, the postal service was quite good and we were able to keep in regular contact with our families at home. Apart from letters, they also kept us supplied with the Guardian Weekly, the Reader's Digest, and occasional copies of the Bristol Evening Post. As we had no radio, this was a very helpful way for us to keep in touch with events outside the village, even if rather belatedly. For Baby, all photos in newspapers were "Daddy," which was especially flattering when they included a photo of Miss World! After a while, some of the village children learnt the word "Daddy" from Helen, and they too would sometimes address me as "Daddy" just as she did. Presumably they did not understand the real meaning. At any rate, Glenys never acted as if she were suspicious!

When I returned from Ahoada to Orupata it was time for a second language session, this time with Bob. While this was going on, Big Helen would be looking after Baby, so we could reckon on relative peace and quiet. After that Glenys would cook some lunch, which usually consisted of rice or macaroni with some meat from a tin, or occasionally from the market. Every now and then a cow was slaughtered in Ahoada, and though the meat was inclined to be on the tough side, Bob had a standing order to buy us some liver whenever he heard about the slaughtering. The local staple was yam, and yam farming was a major activity for many people. Yams are root vegetables, and grow quite large. The season when new yams become available is eagerly anticipated as it means the end of the lean time of the year. We were occasionally given a yam, but never acquired much of a taste for them. They could be boiled and mashed or sliced, but were very solid and seemed to sit heavily after they were eaten. We preferred the smaller coco-yams, which we found tastier. They could be sliced much more easily, and would even make passable chips. There was not much available in the way of greens, though we were often able to get small tomatoes.

After lunch both we and Baby were ready for a siesta. We had never had an afternoon nap before we went to Africa, but we found the climate in Orupata very enervating, and were now glad to do so. The temperature was almost never below 80 degrees Fahrenheit (about 27 Celsius), and for most of the year there was extremely high humidity. It was not easy to sleep during the heat of the day, and as our verandah was open, children used to gather in the shade there and play – but not always quietly. So we had a gate installed across the verandah entrance. There was no lock on it, but it did help a bit to make the afternoons less noisy. As the temperature went down very little at night, Helen generally woke three or four times and cried out for a drink, so we could not sleep well either. We took it in turns to be on duty for supplying drinks to Helen, so each of us had alternate nights of slightly less disturbed rest, but we were still more than ready for our siestas. In retrospect, the climate was the worst we have ever encountered, and of course the lack of electricity meant that there was no relief to be had from a fan, let alone air conditioning.

After the siesta we would either do some analysis of the language data collected earlier, or go for a walk round the village and try talking to people. In a hot climate much of life is conducted outdoors, so there was never any lack of people to talk to. And having a small child is a sure way of finding something to talk about. At this time of day, Big Helen would do some ironing, a much more complicated procedure when there is no electricity. We had two metal flat-irons, which would be heated alternately over one of the burners of the kerosene stove, then clipped inside a smooth metal base to do the actual ironing. We also had a large piece of hardboard to put over one end of the table to give a smooth, flat surface, and this served as an ironing board. The first hot iron could be used until it cooled off, then the other one would take its place while it was reheated. Ironing all clothes was more important than it may seem, because one of the delights of the Niger Delta was a creature called a tumbu fly. This had a nasty habit of laying its eggs in wet clothing. If the clothes were not thoroughly ironed to destroy any eggs, the egg would hatch when the clothes were worn, and the larva would burrow into the skin of the wearer, creating a sore from which it would emerge when it was ready for the next stage of life. We had encountered one such case while we were in Ghana, and were not keen to experience it ourselves, so ironing was taken very seriously. Happily we never had any problems.

Before darkness fell we would have tea, for which we rapidly established a daily diet of home-made bread, and fresh fruit salad, made from the local fruits readily and cheaply available the whole year round. Glenys had a special square tin that fitted over the top of one of the kerosene burners, and this served as an oven in which she could bake bread, which she did regularly about twice a week. The yeast would be kneaded into the dough, and the mixture put in a bowl covered by a cloth on a stool in the garden to rise. It was impossible to control the oven heat accurately, so the bread varied from one baking to the next. Sometimes it was just right and sometimes it was coated with soot, but we just brushed it off and ate the bread anyway. At first we had bought sliced bread in Ahoada market, in a wrapper that proudly proclaimed "Wrapped for Hygiene." Then one day I happened to see the bread being sliced with a rusty old knife and wrapped by grubby hands, so thereafter we decided that occasional soot was the lesser of two risks. For Baby the bread was usually spiced up with Marmite, the substance that seems to distinguish the British from all other varieties of expatriate, and whose name was firmly entrenched in her vocabulary from an early stage.

In the evening we would bath Helen and put her to bed, then do more language work in preparation for the following day, or write letters. We would take our own baths as best we could in the plastic baby bath, and were never late going to bed. For lighting we had a kerosene pressure lamp, and several small lamps with wicks. The pressure lamp we had brought with us and the small lamps came, via Ahoada market, from Eastern Germany. The manufacturer's symbol on the base of the lamp was a bat, so these were always known as bat lamps. (We still have one rusting quietly away in the shed at the bottom of the garden.) The pressure lamp gave out a lot of heat as well as a good light, so I fixed up a high shelf to put it on. This shed the light further and removed the unwanted heat. Since we had no mosquito netting on the windows, the light attracted all manner of insects, many of them unfamiliar to us. Among them were plenty of moths of various shapes, sizes, and colours, the like of which we have never seen since. Once the light was out we enjoyed the company of the many fireflies that flitted around, twinkling amicably in the darkness.

Interruptions were part of the warp and woof of village life. Within the first few weeks of our stay interruptions from people included passing missionaries bringing a message or some fruit, or some furniture they didn't need, or neighbours coming to sell fruit, eggs, and occasionally a chicken or a fish, or to bring a sick child for inspection and advice, or to show us some bush animal we were not familiar with, or just to greet us. Older children would offer to draw a bucket of water from the well for us, for which the reward was an ice-cube. Ice-cubes were outside their previous experience, and ownership of one clearly conferred a considerable, if transient, prestige. Such a low temperature elicited excited shrieks of theatrical agony as they passed the cube from hand to hand until it melted. The bolder spirits would even dare to suck it and risk a frozen tongue.

Some of the more beguiling interruptions came from officialdom. One day a man from the Federal Office of Statistics came around conducting some sort of census. We were happy to co-operate and invited him into the house, where we all sat solemnly around the table. One of his standard questions was how old we were. When Glenys told him she was 30, he laid his pen down and stared at her doubtfully.

"Madam," he declared, "That I cannot believe." We tried to assure him that in England, unlike in Nigeria, everybody knew precisely when they were born, and she really was 30 years old. He remained unconvinced, so she told him that in England, a lady would not normally admit to being over 21. He beamed happily at us. "21," he repeated. "That I can believe." So 21 became Glenys' official age for the purposes of the Federal Office of Statistics. Presumably some of their other statistics were equally reliable.

Another day, we were surprised to see half a dozen men charging purposefully past our kitchen window heading for the jungle, while the womenfolk of neighbouring houses stood around laughing. This was not a normal occurrence, and since there was no evidence of a sudden epidemic of diarrhoea in the village, we sought an explanation. It turned out that some officials had come to collect an annual poll tax of one pound per head for adult males, so those who were unable or unwilling to pay were making themselves scarce until the tax collectors had passed on elsewhere.

There were some difficult decisions to make about how far we could become involved in the social life of the village. Because of our links with Reverend, we were associated in people's minds with the Southern Baptist Mission, and this brought some advantages and some disadvantages. Certainly the Baptists had made us feel very welcome, and we regularly attended the Baptist church. But we were in the village for the purpose of language learning, and with only one year available, we could not allow ourselves to be distracted by too much involvement in church matters. I was sometimes invited to preach at the village service, but accepted only if there was a good reason, such as Okpara's occasional absence at a church conference or training weekend. Although there would be interpretation into Ekpeye, we discovered soon enough that a sermon preached in "latingramma" would not be fully understood even by the interpreter, and would be completely lost on most of the congregation. The fragility of communication by interpreter was vividly illustrated to us one day when our landlord came to see us, looking rather anxious. He had heard that I was going to England for the weekend, and wanted to make sure I was coming back. What on earth either of us could have said that led to this misunderstanding we never found out.

On the other side of the ledger, being regarded as Baptist missionaries meant that we were expected to behave according to the standards for which the genuine missionaries were well known. Since this included total abstinence from alcohol, we had the perfect excuse for abstaining from the local hooch, palm wine. Whenever there was a festival in the village, there would be a gathering in the *unama*, the village "playground," an open plaza some distance from our home, and we would go along to watch for a while. There would be dancing, in which men formed one circle and women another two inside the first one, and the three circles would gyrate anticlockwise to the monotonous beating of drums. There was no special clothing worn, and as far as we could judge no particular skill required, except perhaps from the drummer. Palm wine was served in abundance, a liquid of singularly uninviting appearance. It was a sickly pallid grey colour, and to us it had an uncanny resemblance to washing up water after the washing up is finished and the suds have disappeared. Moreover it was liberally spiked with drowned wasps. We were always offered some, often with a mischievous grin, and at such times we were particularly glad to shelter under the umbrella of Baptist abstinence.

A different kind of dilemma arose from Glenys' medical qualification. We were aware that if it became widely known, she would be inundated with requests for medical help. She was not registered to practice in Nigeria, and in any case we had nothing more than a first aid box with a few basic essentials in it. Occasionally she did dispense first aid, especially where children were involved, but since there was a perfectly good Seventh Day Adventist hospital only five miles the other side of Ahoada along the main road, we did not feel that we had a heavy responsibility in this sphere. On one occasion not long after we arrived, a mother who was one of our neighbours brought to us a small child with several nasty abscesses on its body. Glenys could only advise the mother to take the child to the hospital, but it seemed she was too poor to afford even the modest fees there. As it happened, some Baptist missionaries called on us next day on their way to Joinkrama, and we were able to send the mother and child with them to the hospital there at our expense. They returned about ten days later with the child well recovered after a course of antibiotics, and our total medical bill was less than six pounds. After a few days the mother came along and shyly presented us with three eggs as her way of saying thank you. We felt our money had been well spent.

Chapter 5
Village People and Village Churches

We lived at one end of Orupata, the end furthest from the main road, and our main contacts were naturally with our immediate neighbours. A few yards from the front of our compound was a broad depression in the ground two or three feet deep, which we came to call the swamp. It was not actually a swamp, and after a while we discovered that it was not a natural feature at all. It had in fact been created by people digging away the earth to make the mud walls of their houses. Their houses were all built on the same pattern, oblong in shape with a single wooden door and one or at most two small windows with wooden shutters. The shutters were always closed at night, so it must have been very stuffy to sleep inside with no ventilation of any kind. The houses had a wooden framework made from trees cut in the forest, and mud walls, with the mud often dug from the swamp. The roof was made of palm leaves woven together into a thatch thick enough to keep out the rain in the wet season. The size of the house varied with the size of the family, but the basic design was the same everywhere. People who prospered might put on a roof of galvanised iron, known locally as "pan," but Mr. Ebeku was one of the very few people who had a house built of concrete blocks like the one we lived in.

The neighbours we saw most of were those to the left of our house, the side where there was no hedge. The neighbour we became aware of soonest was a cheerful little boy called Chika, who was about a year older than our Helen, and lived in the next house but one. The children mostly ran around naked until they were about 12 years old, and Chika was no exception. He was often among the children who made their way to our verandah and he and Helen quickly became friends. His mother, an attractive young woman who didn't look as if she was far out of her teens, was always known as "*ina Chika*" ("Mother-of-Chika") and she and her smaller baby (called Lady) were also often to be seen on the verandah. Her husband, Stephen, was not much in evidence and, to our perception, did not seem to be greatly missed. Perhaps he was working elsewhere and only able to get home infrequently. When he was home, he came across as a somewhat curmudgeonly fellow, and we were not entirely surprised on one occasion when we heard that Chika's mother and the baby had run away, presumably back to her own mother in some other village. Stephen was left to look after Chika, perhaps to teach him a lesson. After a week or so Mother-of-Chika returned, and the incident was not repeated, at least not while we were there.

Beyond Chika's house was another house at right angles to it in which lived a boy called Jones. However Ekpeye did not have words ending in the sounds "ns" so the "n" was not usually pronounced, and to us the name sounded more like Jose. Jones was about seven years old, old enough to have started school, so we saw less of him. When he was around, he was a mischievous imp, but never in a malicious way. Beyond Jones lived a man called Meeting, with a small son called Young. Meeting earned his living by carrying pillion passengers on his bicycle, and cycled, so he told us, up to a hundred miles a day. How he managed such distances, if he really did, in that climate was hard to imagine, but he certainly had well developed calf muscles!

In the very next house to ours lived a plump, smiling little girl of about five called Anti, with her mother, who was inevitably called Mother-of-Anti. For some reason, we also knew her own name, which was Alice. There was no man around in that house, and Okpara explained that her husband was "gone to Spanish." We were not at all sure what this meant, but eventually discovered that he had joined a group of migrant workers on the rubber plantations on the island of Fernando Po. At that time it was under Spanish colonial administration, but is now part of the independent country known as Equatorial

Guinea. "Father-of-Anti" never appeared during our time in Orupata, but after a few months Anti and her mother disappeared, going to join him in "Spanish." During their absence, their house was occupied by a single man, but that is another story, to be told later.

The Ekpeye people did their cooking outdoors over wood fires. It was the job of the women to collect firewood in the forest, to which they would go in groups of three or four. When a suitable amount had been collected, it would be tied in heavy bundles, and the women would help one another lift the bundles onto their heads to carry home. We were amazed at how much they could carry, though not surprised to hear that back trouble was a common complaint among older women. There was nothing around the fires to protect small children from accidents. One day Anti slipped and fell into the fire, sustaining a nasty burn on one hand. Alice brought her tearful little girl to Glenys, who was able to use some of our first aid kit to dress and bandage the wound. Anti recovered well and was none the worse for her misadventure. A few weeks later we woke up one morning to find Alice busy renovating the mud walls of our latrine. It turned out to be the time of year (after the end of the wet season) when people regularly carried out this kind of maintenance on the mud walls of their houses. Although the latrine was pretty new and did not really need much attention, this was Alice's way of saying thank you for Glenys' medical care for Anti. We were very touched by such a practical, affordable and culturally appropriate way of showing gratitude.

Between Alice's house and ours another small house was constructed during our stay, so we were able to witness the process of building, making the frame with "stick" from the forest, weaving the palm thatch, and constructing the mud walls. It was all very DIY, but used completely appropriate technology, and cost very little apart from physical effort. This was spread among a number of friends and relatives and accompanied by quite a bit of jollity. Only the wooden door, padlock, and window shutters needed to be made or bought for cash. The occupant of this house was a quiet young man called Seven, presumably because he was the seventh child in his family. In due course we got to know him quite well, and to appreciate his skill as a story teller.

Behind our compound lived a family with a little boy of about six who had a deformed leg, and consequently a bad limp. This lad was named Good, and seldom could a name have been less appropriate. If there was any mischief going on among the children, Good was always at the centre of it. One of his favourite tricks was throwing stones onto the metal roof of our house, especially during our attempted siesta time. One day I managed to creep up on him unseen and catch him. He hollered as if he was about to be eaten. I frog-marched him through our house into the walled back yard, from which he could not escape, and left him there for ten minutes to contemplate his sins. Mother-of-Good heard his yells, came to investigate, and was highly amused by his incarceration. He was eventually released slightly but only temporarily chastened, and hardly a reformed character. Father-of-Good was the owner of a ladder, and this made him a very useful person if anything was dropped down the well, or if the well needed cleaning. The ladder was not like any ladders we had seen before. It consisted of a single long bamboo upright with shorter cross-pieces tied at suitable intervals as rungs. It was a precarious looking contraption, but very suitable for putting down the well, where it could never do worse than lean a little to one side, and the climber was always able to lever it straight again.

To the left of our house, behind a row of plantains, lived a man called Enoch and his family. There was one older girl who married while we were there and a younger one who was often among the crowd of children in the vicinity of our house. There was also a little boy of about three with a name that to us was very strange. He was called Manager. Enoch explained to us that when the boy was born he was working for Shell, away from the Ekpeye area, and the manager allowed him some leave to return home and see his family. So in gratitude, the boy was named Manager. Enoch was a man who gave the impression of competence and reliability, and we came to respect his opinions and advice when it was offered.

After some while Enoch got another job away somewhere, his wife being pregnant again. When she delivered this time, it was twins, which was considered a very bad omen in that area. She had had twins when Manager was born, but the other baby was very small at birth, and had died quickly without any neglect. But now Enoch's wife came under considerable pressure to follow tradition and neglect one of the new twins so that he died. So Glenys visited her daily for a while until Enoch came home. Enoch was a practising Roman Catholic and was determined to resist this kind of pressure and to keep both twins, so to support his wife and children he gave up his job altogether and returned to the village. He was very grateful for the support Glenys had given, and told us that he did not want his wife to be "confused by the silly women in the village." In terms of the village economy, giving up a job was a major sacrifice, and one could not but respect such a man. His stand was rewarded, and up to the time we left, both the twins were flourishing.

Just beyond Enoch lived a man called Patrick who was an Igbo. He was living with an Ekpeye girl, though they were not married. The girl delivered a baby daughter during the year, and Patrick was as pleased as punch, informing us, "I go marry de modda." Presumably the reasoning was that since the girl was proved to be fertile, she was now worth marrying. Patrick could often be seen carrying the baby proudly round to show to anyone who cared to look. Indeed it was not uncommon for men in the village to be seen carrying small babies and playing with them. In fact it was probably more common there than it was in England at that time.

Another character who was often in evidence, and who lived in a house beyond Enoch's, was a man who introduced himself to us as the Duke of Edinburgh. We were not sure at first whether this was some kind of joke, but people did seem to call him Duke. Whether his real name was either Edinburgh or Duke we never discovered. Had he been younger, born about the time that the then Princess Elizabeth married, and Prince Philip was created Duke of Edinburgh, then that might well have been his real name. But he was older than that, and we were inclined to think that his "peerage" was self-bestowed. Not having much alternative, we joined in calling him Duke, especially when he had had a little too much palm wine.

In addition to the people who lived near us, there were the occasional vendors who came round with their wares. The ones we were most aware of would come crying out "*Mai mai*" in a very nasal tone. *Mai mai* was a foodstuff and was something we had never seen before. We were never sure what it was made from. It was soft and greyish white, looking a bit like yoghurt, but it could not have been made from milk as milk products were unknown in the area. It did not look to us very attractive, and the sellers did not seem to expect us to buy it, so we did not disappoint them.

Men in the village usually wore a pair of shorts, and if they were trendy, a string vest. For some reason a string vest was a sign of being "with it" in those days. Most men had a shirt or two, but shirts were generally reserved for formal occasions, as were long trousers. Many people went barefoot, or wore cheap sandals. Shoes were seldom seen. Little boys generally ran around naked until they went to school at about six years old. There was no school in Orupata, and the children had to walk the two miles each way to Ahoada for school. The smallest boys like Jones would leave the village naked, with their shorts folded neatly and carried on top of their head together with their slate. They would put their shorts on only when they got near the school, and would take them off again when they were on the way home.

Small girls also went naked until they started school, when they would begin to wear a loose dress. Girls who had left school and were not yet married continued to wear a dress, or a blouse and skirt, often a very short skirt. Married women with babies usually wore an ankle length wrap-around cloth, but went topless so that the baby could be fed easily and at any time. The baby was tied in a cloth on mother's back when small, and usually sat on mother's hip when it was a bit bigger. When mother produced the next baby, an older sibling or cousin would take on the job of carrying the previous one. Sometimes children (usually girls) of not more than four or five would have a smaller child on their hip, and as a rule they managed very professionally. Not to be outdone, Baby Helen often went round with her Teddy Bear tied onto her back with a coloured cloth. On village market days, young mothers who normally went topless might put on a bra to go out in – not a blouse, just a bra. Possession of such an exotic item was evidently a status symbol.

Not far beyond the swamp across an open space was the largest church in the village, the United National African Church (UNA). It was the largest building because it had the largest congregation. It was not linked with any western church or mission, but was one of the many indigenous churches that had sprung up all over Africa in reaction to foreign domination. The big attraction of the UNA was that it made a significant concession to traditional culture by permitting polygamy. The pastor of this church was a Mr. Izagi, and he would occasionally wander across to our house for a chat. He had reasonable English, and generally preferred to practice his English rather than encourage us to speak Ekpeye. We maintained a friendly relationship with him, but despite our curiosity, we felt that because of the polygamy issue it would not be prudent for us to attend a service in his church – not that he ever tried to persuade us to do so.

Not far beyond Mother-of-Chika's house was another small church that had services only at infrequent intervals. This was the Roman Catholic Church, and the services were infrequent because there was only one priest in the area, and he had many villages to visit. One Sunday there was a harvest festival in the Catholic Church, so of course all the children went there to observe the spectacle. We had not been told about it in advance, but after a while we became aware that Baby Helen was nowhere to be seen, and neither were the other children. When we inquired we were told about the service, and made our way round to the Catholic Church just as the service was ending, and all the children, Helen among them, surged forward to be sprinkled with holy water. The priest, who had not known of our presence in Orupata, was astonished to find an unaccompanied white toddler among his flock! So when the ceremony was over, we retrieved Helen and introduced ourselves to the priest, a large extrovert Irishman called Father Flynn. He joined us for a snack, and in the course of time we became quite friendly with him, of which more anon.

Between the UNA church and the main sealed road through the village lay a small market place, where there was a market every four days. One day as I was cycling through the market, I was called aside by the Market

Master, and politely but sternly warned that cycling through the market was forbidden, and if I did it again, I would be fined five shillings. A very reasonable safety precaution, and I took care not to sin again! Near the market stood another little church. This was an Anglican church, and services took place there about as irregularly as in the Catholic church. There were very few Anglicans, and those that there were seemed to be people from other areas. I went on one occasion to a service conducted by a lay reader, and found that the service was neither in Ekpeye nor English, but in Igbo, so I understood next to nothing, and did not repeat the experiment.

At the furthest part of the village from our house was yet another church, where the Seventh Day Adventists met. Nobody from our end of the village seemed to attend that church, and as the services were naturally on Saturdays when we were otherwise engaged, we had virtually no contact with it. However about five miles the other side of Ahoada there was the Seventh Day Adventist hospital, with several foreign medical staff, and as time went by we did get to know some of them. The hospital had a good name, and our relationships with the staff there were always cordial.

Just on the other side of the main road was the Baptist church that we normally went to. It was a fair-sized building, larger than the Catholic and Anglican buildings, and like most of the houses in the village constructed of a wooden frame with a thatched roof and mud walls. In this case the walls were only half the height of the building, so that when the church was full, there was still a little breeze blowing through. The services took place every week, usually led by Okpara. They consisted of the normal sort of mixture of hymns, prayers, a Bible reading and a sermon. The hymns were mostly English hymns, sung with no musical accompaniment, and not infrequently to the wrong tune - not just a tune unfamiliar to us, but a tune whose metre was quite different from that of the words. This was galling enough for me, but much worse for Glenys, who could not only play the piano competently, but was also blessed (or cursed) with absolute pitch.

Most of the service was in Ekpeye except for the Bible reading. No part of the Bible had been published in Ekpeye, so Okpara would read the lesson from the King James Version in English, then give his own ad hoc interpretation into Ekpeye. Our comprehension of Ekpeye was not sufficient for us to follow all the details, and this was probably just as well. We knew that Okpara's grasp of English was not up to the King James language level, so his interpretations were almost certainly idiosyncratic to say the least. He would sometimes give a summary of his sermon in English for our benefit, and the one we remember best was about two characters called Rebecca and Lucy, both apparently male! Rebecca wanted to borrow Lucy's hoe to "go farm" and work on a Sunday.

Lucy agreed to lend the hoe, so Rebecca went to work on the farm, and God was not pleased. The moral of the story was clearly that on Sunday one should give attendance at church priority over everyday concerns, however important. But the story was presented as a Bible story, and brought home to us the difficulty that many pastors like Okpara labour under by not having a Bible in a language that they can readily understand. At one level, the sermon had its amusing side, but at a deeper level, it underlined the importance of Bible translation for a strong and well-founded church life. Despite Okpara's undoubted sincerity, he casually told us one day that in his spare time he ran a lottery – not quite a typical sideline for a Baptist pastor!

Our rent was due once a month, but because Elijah, the landlord, was not literate, paying it involved a visit to Mr. Ebeku so that he could be a witness and ensure that a receipt was written. Finding a moment when Elijah and Mr. Ebeku were both free was not always easy, and we were not sorry when after a few months Elijah rather diffidently asked if we could see our way to paying off the whole of the rest of our year's rent at one go. We were not averse to this, though it took a while to organise the requisite amount of cash. It was in fact as a result of our willingness to pay in advance that Elijah was able to have ceilings put in the house, so there were benefits all round. The actual owner of our house was Elijah's brother

Simpson, and he called on us one day when he was home on leave from his job in Lagos. He inspected the house, and was apparently satisfied that we were looking after it well enough for him. Then he inspected the garden, with its sugar cane, and the four kitchens at the far end. Turning to me, Simpson muttered darkly, "Many wives, much trouble." In some contexts such a remark might have been taken as a joke, but somehow I felt that he was speaking from the depths of unhappy experience, so I just agreed with him as solemnly as I could, and remained monogamous.

Elijah had two unmarried teenaged daughters, and they would come to the house from time to time to keep an eye on the plants growing in the back garden, and to take some of the plentiful sugar cane. This usually meant a small piece of sugar cane for Helen, which like the other children, she loved to suck and chew. In the absence of sweets and chocolates, we did not begrudge her this little luxury. Like most young women, Elijah's daughters had their hair done in a way we had not seen before. The whole head would be divided by partings into little squares, and the hair in each square was tied into a small plait. The girl would end up with a dozen or more of these little plaits pointing in different directions. It was a complicated hair-do which could only be done by somebody else, and girls were often to be seen, especially on a Sunday afternoon, happily engaged in the social ritual of doing each other's hair.

When girls married, it was the custom for the groom's family to provide a "bride price." This was not at all the same thing as "buying" the bride, but was rather a seal of the contract between two families, and a stabilising factor in keeping the marriage together. It could still be a heavy financial burden for the groom's family, and there was an official government limit of thirty pounds to the amount that could be requested for a bride price, though this was unenforceable and was often honoured in the breach. People would sometimes ask how much bride price I had had to give for Glenys, and an explanation that there was no bride price system in England was always met with incredulity. People thought I just did not want to admit that I had paid more than she was worth. So I took to telling them I had paid "*shen isabo li shishi*," seven shillings and sixpence, the price of a marriage licence in England at the time we took the plunge. This answer was not untrue at one level, and avoided vain attempts to explain cultural differences. Moreover it changed the equation considerably. Questioners now considered that for such a modest and affordable investment, I had actually obtained a good bargain, a conclusion I saw no reason to dispute. As one man responded thoughtfully and not without surprise, "And she can read too!" A bargain indeed.

From time to time other local visitors dropped in. One man took great interest in Helen's Teddy Bear, and after a close inspection, pronounced it to be female on the grounds that its anatomy lacked any distinctively male components. We did not argue. Bob's mother from Ekpena village called in to see us when she was visiting Orupata to comfort a bereaved relative, and Helen's father from Obholobholo village also called in one day on his way to town. Helen was one of four daughters, and it was very important to a man to have a son. Nevertheless we were rather taken aback when Helen returned from her weekend at home on one occasion and casually announced that her father had taken a second wife. We were even more surprised to learn that the wife he had taken was a girl of about Helen's age who already had a son born out of wedlock. Helen herself showed no signs of surprise or disapproval. When we asked Reverend about the logic of the situation, he explained how the fact that the girl already had a son proved that she was fertile, and even if she did not bear another son to Helen's father, well, by marrying her he had already acquired her existing son as his own, so his problem was solved. This was an object lesson to us in the need to try to understand people's actions in terms of their own value systems, rather than evaluate them too hastily by ours.

Among our visitors we were one day honoured by a visit from the Eze of the whole Ekpeye people, who lived in Ihuabha village, the other side of Ahoada. The term "*eze*" was often given the equivalent "king" when people spoke English, but perhaps Paramount Chief would be less misleading. He was accompanied by another Chief, called somewhat unexpectedly, Jones. We learnt that the Eze had at some stage in his career been a government interpreter, and so he was interested to hear about our work. As it happened, the very next day I met the Eze again in Ahoada as I was passing the house of the local Member of Parliament. I was summoned into the house to meet the MP, a very jovial man who had studied at the University of Exeter. He introduced me to another man with the words, "He stood against me at the last election." Then with a roar of laughter, he added, "And he lost his deposit." Neither man seemed to bear any ill will however, and in the ensuing entirely amicable conversation I gathered that the other man was actually a supporter of the MP who only stood against him to split the opposition! Politicians have their bags of tricks the world over.

Around Christmas time, many people who lived outside the Ekpeye area would return home if they could, and not a few came to greet us and to satisfy their curiosity about us. One such was a young man by the name of Nathan who was on leave from the army. He informed us that as it was New Year, his grandmother and another older lady (who turned out to be Okpara's mother) were going to burn their jujus. We were invited to the ceremony, and to have lunch with him afterwards. We were not at all sure what would happen at the ceremony, or how important it was, or what exactly the jujus were. At any rate they were something to do with non-Christian religious activity, and burning them might be a token of a new Christian commitment. We went along therefore with great interest to see what would happen. It appeared that the ceremony had some connection with the Baptist church, as a group of the church members were in attendance, singing much of the time lustily if not quite harmoniously. The jujus were collected and taken to the burial ground and burnt. As far as we could see they consisted of feathers, a piece of metal, a wooden stool, and some thatch. What their significance was, and what burning them meant was never explained to us. This was an entirely indigenous ceremony at which we were only invited observers. We did not like to ask too many questions in case they were taken to imply disapproval, but perhaps we should have been bolder in our search for understanding.

Nathan's invitation was the one and only invitation we had to eat in a local home, and from our observations of how and what the village people cooked and ate, we were a little apprehensive. We need not have been. Nathan provided rice, a very peppery fish soup, and plantain, all of which he cooked himself. There was also Pepsi-Cola to drink, and finally a cup of tea. Moreover we were seated at a table indoors with individual bowls and cutlery rather than sitting around outside on stools and helping ourselves from a common pot. Probably few people in Orupata could have provided such exotic trappings to a meal, and presumably Nathan gained some kudos from having us as his guests. Unfortunately his leave did not last long enough for us to have an opportunity to return his hospitality, and we never saw him again.

Chapter 6
Visiting Other Villages

Occasionally I made an excursion to some other village. The first was to Okporowo, a village not far off the main road to Abua. The reason for going there was to renew acquaintance with the first Ekpeye man to qualify as a medical doctor, Friday by name. We had actually met him in England before leaving, and were glad to see him again after his return home. I was accompanied to Okporowo by Bob, and by Gibson, a relative of Friday's, in whose shop in Ahoada Bob had served some sort of apprenticeship as a radio mechanic. As was the custom, Friday offered us all a drink, and the choice was between bottled beer and probably unboiled well water. I have never acquired a taste for beer, but in the circumstances it seemed the lesser of two evils, and I was far enough away from Orupata to be temporarily beyond the penumbra of the Baptist Mission!

Some time later we received an invitation to Friday's wedding. He was marrying an Abuan girl, a nursing sister called Vicky, whom we had also met in England. The wedding was to be held at the Catholic Cathedral in Onitsha, 150 miles from Ahoada, but we received the invitation only two days before the actual ceremony, so unfortunately we had no possibility of attending.

Bob had a great respect for his father, who he told me was "At least one hundred years old." Since Bob himself was only 15, this seemed a little unlikely, but I deemed it prudent to investigate before disputing the claim. So one day I went with Bob to his home in Ekpena village, a mile or so from Ahoada on the other side of the Sambreiro river. I was made welcome, and was able to convince myself if not Bob that, venerable as his father might be, he was not a day over sixty. Father himself was more than ready to don his ceremonial dress as a chief for me to take a photo. The dress consisted of a long robe and a walking stick, and rather incongruously, a pith helmet that was presumably a relic of colonial times. Bob also showed me his father's juju house, which contained a stick with a face carved on it, and sometimes also a wooden stool, some feathers and some of the old money. This took the form of metal bars in the shape of horseshoes, known as manilas. Modern money also found uses other than economic. The Nigerian penny coins had a hole in the middle, and so could be carried on a string threaded through them. One of the babies in Bob's extended family had such a necklace of penny coins around its neck as a decoration.

The *unama* in Ekpena contained a structure unlike anything in Orupata, a two story building raised from the ground on stilts, which Bob referred to as "the playhouse." On certain occasions special dances took place in the shaded area under the building. In front of it were a series of upright poles on which awnings could be hung to give added shade to spectators.

As Ekpena village was on the river, people there could go to their farms by boat rather than on foot as in Orupata. As we crossed the river on a canoe, Bob proudly pointed out to me how careful his people were with hygiene. "We always wash downstream from where we get drinking water," he assured me.

"Are there any villages upstream from you?" I asked him, and he confirmed that there were.

"So you drink the water those people have washed in?" His mouth dropped open, as this possibility had obviously never occurred to him before. The distance between villages and the volume of water in the river were such that the risks were probably small, but the incident does show how much we in modern industrial societies take for granted the ready availability of clean water.

A further visit, in the company of Reverend, was to the village of Ihuaba, four miles the other side of Ahoada. There were several reasons for going there. It was the home of the Eze and Chief Jones, who had called on us some time previously, so it was appropriate for me to return their call. It was also the home of a man called Mr. Abu who worked in Lagos, and had called on us during his home leave and invited us to visit him. Thirdly, it was the home village of Augustine, an Ekpeye man we had met in London who had given us three or four sessions of basic Ekpeye instruction while we were still in England. As we cycled along the track, I was surprised to see a small group of men working in the bush completely naked. Nearby was another man in a uniform, and Reverend explained to me that the naked men were inmates of the local prison who were on an outside working party. Depriving them of their clothes for the period of their excursion was a cheap, simple and effective way to deter them from absconding.

When we reached Ihuaba, we found that that there was a juju sacrifice going on that day, so everyone we hoped to see was at home. Chief Jones fed us with bean fritters, alligator pepper, coconut and biscuits, and Mr. Abu with yam and chicken, so we certainly did not go hungry. On this occasion there was no beer on offer, perhaps because Reverend was known to be a Baptist, so we both drank unboiled water, but suffered no ill effects. The only kerfuffle that occurred was when I needed to go to the toilet. All I required was to know which part of the surrounding bush to use, but for my hosts this was not the proper way to treat a European, and eventually I was taken to a house that had a facility similar to ours in Orupata, and honour was satisfied all round.

In making visits like this there were two cultural practices that I had to adapt to. One was the way men shook hands. On releasing hands, somehow they contrived to make a clicking noise with their thumbs. Everybody seemed to be able to do it except me, and try as I might, I never became a proficient thumb-clicker. The other practice was to open a nut called a cola nut and offer a piece to a guest. The cola nut was large as nuts go, about the size of a small apple, and once opened was in two or three segments, with a consistency something like that of a hazel nut. The taste was rather bitter, and I never liked it very much, but eating a piece was part of the ritual of making a guest welcome, and it would have been offensive to refuse.

On a later occasion I cycled with Reverend to his home village of Obholobholo to meet his father, and also to visit Big Helen's family. It was only nine miles from Orupata, partly along the tarmac road towards Mbiama, and the rest on a fairly narrow unsealed track through the bush. Despite the short distance it took almost an hour and a half to get there. The area was fairly remote by Ekpeye standards, and this was a source of teasing between Bob and Helen, enacted largely in English, and probably as much for our benefit as theirs. Bob's village was only a mile or so from Ahoada, so he felt quite metropolitan in comparison with someone from distant Obholobholo, which he dismissed as only a tiny village. In response Helen always referred to her village as "Obholobholo township," but this cut no ice with Bob. He alleged that in the Obholobholo area, the bush was so thick that people had only recently learnt to wear clothes. Helen always rose indignantly to this bait, but because her English was not as fluent as Bob's, he always got the better of these good natured tussles.

The people in Obholobholo certainly were wearing clothes, and we were received very hospitably by both the families we visited, and regaled with Coca Cola and biscuits. As in Abua, there were creeks in Obholobholo, and we visited two different watersides at opposite ends of the village, though at that time of year in the dry season, one of them had no water. The highlight of the visit however was a walk into the forest to inspect a place where Reverend and another pastor had made a fish pond. The pond was connected to the creek, and the idea was that the fish would swim in when the tide was high, and then when the water receded they would be trapped in the pond, to be caught easily when needed. The only drawback to this arrangement was that the fisherman had no chance to boast about "the one that got away." This pond was sited where it was because that particular part of the forest was regarded as "juju bush," the abode of evil spirits and therefore dangerous for people to make fish ponds in. The old man who had accompanied us around the village up to this point excused himself when we headed for the fish pond, saying that he was tired, so fear of the juju was clearly real. Reverend and his friend had deliberately chosen this spot as a demonstration that Christians are guarded by a power greater than that of any evil spirits, and indeed no harm ever befell them. There was in the area a creature that Reverend referred to as an alligator, though in reality alligators are not found in Africa. Presumably it was some kind of crocodile, but although we saw the hole where it was supposed to live, and Reverend poked a long stick in, we saw no sign of the creature itself, rather to my relief. Some days later, however, he did kill a small "alligator" in that very area.

When the time came to leave, we were festooned with gifts. Helen's family gave me five eggs, a stem of bananas and two tins of evaporated milk. Reverend's family added two coconuts and a live hen, so we had more than enough goods for two bicycles, and the return journey home was even slower than the outward one. I was more than ready to stop at Upatabo village on the way to buy some soft drinks in the little market there.

The hen was probably intended for us to eat, but we were too soft-hearted to slaughter her, and so became involuntary livestock owners. Baby Helen was delighted to have her own "birbie" around the house. Following Reverend's instructions, we kept the hen in the back garden for three days with a long string tied around one leg, then removed it and hesitantly let her out. She perked up at once, and set off to explore the neighbourhood. In the evening she came back of her own accord, and took up her perch on the window sill, from where she could watch our comings and goings. That was all right with us, but after a few days, she grew presumptuous, and invited herself inside the house. As long as she kept to the floor, we let her alone, but then she decided she wanted to patrol the dining table. At the time we were constructing a dictionary file, writing Ekpeye words on flimsy paper slips for filing in alphabetical order. This was a tedious process, and when she landed on the table, her wings sent the carefully sorted paper slips flying in all directions. So we drew the line and ejected her, to the sound of much outraged squawking.

On another occasion when she had invaded the table and was being chased off it, she nearly fell into the baby bath, which was ready to receive its rightful occupant. Helen got quite indignant, and ran about shouting "Baf, baf." But as I chased the squawking hen outside, Helen relented and murmured "*Ekw'ikwa-o*" – "Don't cry" in Ekpeye! Eventually the hen grudgingly accepted that the table was off limits, but the first time she was put outside, she showed her displeasure by returning to her perch on the window sill – this time with her tail towards us!

We hoped she would provide a regular supply of eggs, but we had to wait quite a long time. She was visited in due course by various avian suitors, and subsequently laid some eggs, but did so somewhere in the swamp, and we never found them. Wherever they were, she managed to hatch at least one of them, and for a short time was followed around by a single chick. But one day the chick began to look peeky and next morning it was dead, so the hen was on her own again. I buried it quickly before Baby Helen could see it. The second time the hen laid, it was in the back garden, so we were able to keep a closer eye on things. She had to leave the eggs for a while each day to go and forage for food, so when she was away, we crept out and pencilled the figure 1 on the first, then 2 on the second, and so on. When she laid the fourth, we wrote a 4 on it, and removed number 1 for our own use. She got up to about a dozen before she stopped laying, and never seemed to realise that despite her constant efforts, the number of eggs in the clutch never exceeded three. Once it was clear that the laying had stopped, we removed the last three eggs. She looked a bit puzzled when she came back, but did not seem unduly upset. So by this unscrupulous trickery we did have some profit from our unexpected venture into animal husbandry.

At least we knew where these eggs had come from and how old they were. Eggs were among the goods offered to us regularly in the village, and we had to learn to distinguish between the good ones and the bad ones. Inevitably we failed a few times at the beginning, then Okpara showed us how to tell the difference. The method he taught us was to put them into a bowl of water. If they sank, they were good, and if they floated they were bad. This procedure may be well known today, but it was new to us at the time. It worked, and sometimes would-be vendors were disappointed when our new found skill showed that all their eggs were bad. On one occasion Glenys offered to open all the eggs in front of the vendor, and to buy them if they were good. To her surprise, the offer was accepted. The eggs were duly opened and every one was indeed bad, so the vendor went away a sadder and a wiser man.

Chapter 7
Local Europeans

Before we went to live in Nigeria, we had expected that we would end up somewhere pretty far removed from other Europeans, but Orupata was not as isolated as we had anticipated. The longer we stayed, the more Europeans we came across, though our contacts with them were at most intermittent. The other members of SIL, Ian and Amelia from Abua, and Elaine and Joy from Joinkrama would drop in on us if they were passing our way, and various members of the Southern Baptist Mission at Joinkrama would also call in from time to time. The ones we saw most often were the Green family, who took us one day into Port Harcourt, the nearest large town, about fifty miles away. There we saw the big shops, and indulged ourselves in the luxury of a bar of chocolate. Some years later the Greens were involved in a serious road accident while on leave in the USA, and were unable to return to Nigeria, but we remember their kindness with gratitude.

Once or twice we were visited by Herb, the missionary we had met on our first day in Ahoada. He made visits to the delta area from time to time, and quickly found out where we were living. The first time he came, we had no advance notice of his arrival, and I was chatting with our neighbour Patrick as Herb's van came past the Orupata market, and turned towards our house. Seeing that the van was driven by a white man, Patrick observed with no surprise in his voice, "Ah, yo brodda has come." Thus we were introduced to the very African concept of "expanding brotherhood." If you are in your own village, your brother is a blood relative. If you are in another village, your brother is anyone from your home village. If you are in Enugu, your brother is anyone from Ekpeye. If you are in Lagos, your brother is anyone from Eastern Nigeria. If you are in a neighbouring country, your brother is anyone from Nigeria. If you are in England, your brother is anyone from Africa. Therefore since we were the only white people living in a Nigerian village, any other white person was our brother. The fact that Herb came from Canada and we had only ever set eyes on him once before was totally irrelevant! We were of course very happy to see him and have him stay overnight. He was in the process of training a Nigerian colleague called Godwin to take over his work, and the next time he came Godwin was with him. In due course Herb went on leave, and we were very happy that Godwin felt comfortable to come and stay with us on his own from then on. The Christian concept of brotherhood is even more expansive than the African one. Godwin did not look very old, but as we got to know him better, we were surprised to learn that he was the father of seven children, with another on the way. He also told us that he had been in the army during the Second World War, and had served in Burma, so he must have been older than we had realised.

The most flamboyant European in the Ahoada area was Fr. Flynn, who had evidently kissed the Blarney stone, and kept us entertained with a ceaseless flow of blarney whenever we saw him. He told us that he was a sports enthusiast, and loved to play rugby "whenever I think the Bishop will not find out." In keeping with his build, he played as a forward, and told us with a twinkle in his eye that during his last game, he was a little disconcerted to find one of his parishioners on the touchline, a lady who was the wife of one of the other players. But the worst reaction he got from her was the gentle rebuke, "Watch your language in the scrum there, Fr. Flynn."

When Fr. Flynn visited us, he particularly enjoyed the bread Glenys had baked, which he declared to be almost as good as the bread his mother used to bake in Ireland when he was a boy. So from time to time, I would drop a loaf in to his house in Ahoada. Most of the Roman Catholics in the Ahoada area were Igbos, and Igbo was the language Fr. Flynn had studied when he first arrived in Nigeria. One day when I called on him with some bread, he was dissatisfied with something or other that his houseboy had done, or not done, and I had to listen while he gave the lad a dressing down in Igbo. I did not understand Igbo, but it was apparent that the lad understood no more of it than I did. What was clear was that Fr. Flynn's Irish brogue was as much in evidence when he spoke Igbo as when he spoke English, and I had to have some sympathy for the errant, baffled houseboy.

Fr. Flynn was aware of the need for more local men to be trained as priests, but he was very reserved about the effects of sending them overseas for training. As he colourfully put it, "You send some of these young fellows off to Rome for a couple of years and when they come back, you'd not find a mitre to fit them." Not all the changing attitudes advocated by the recently concluded Second Vatican Council had yet percolated through to Ahoada! Shortly before we left, Fr. Flynn went on leave, and was replaced by Fr. O'Connell. Our overlap time with him was brief so we did not get to know him as well as we had Fr. Flynn.

One day Mr. Lock, one of the Baptist missionaries, took us out to the Seventh Day Adventist hospital at Elele, five miles from Ahoada, to meet the foreign personnel there. The doctor and his wife, Samuel and Bernice, were African Americans, and there was also an English family on the staff, Harry and Esther with their three children. We were very pleased to make their acquaintance, and also relieved that we never needed their help, at least not medically. Samuel was an accomplished pianist and had a fine piano which he even managed to keep in tune, no small feat in the hot and humid climate.

Through Harry and Esther, we learnt that there was another English family living in Ahoada, Roy and Alicia, with their three boys. Before long we met them, and found that Roy was a roads engineer, working on the extension to Yenagoa, deeper into the Niger delta, of the sealed road that ran through Ahoada and Orupata. He told us that when the road reached the Orashi river at Mbiama, there was enough money left either to build a bridge across the river, or to continue the road on the other side of the river. Since there was already a pontoon bridge operating across the river that was well able to cope with the relatively light traffic, it made a lot more sense to continue the road on the other side of the river, and it was the construction of this road that he was working on. One of his tasks was to test the quality of the cement used in the road, and ensure that sand and cement were mixed in appropriate proportions. Since cement was in high demand, there was a tendency for too much sand to be used, and for bags of cement to disappear mysteriously from time to time.

One day we had a pleasant surprise when a car arrived outside our house driven by a white woman on her own. She proved to be Kay Williamson, an English scholar of the languages of the Niger Delta from the University of Ibadan in Western Nigeria. She had been at school with Amelia, so was of our own generation, and we found her very easy company. But because she had fair hair, when I took her for a walk around Orupata people kept asking me if she was my mother. Fortunately she did not understand what they were saying. That was a vivid experience of the difficulty that people often have in estimating the ages of other people from a different ethnic group. But I have no excuse for complacency, for since then I have had several instances of people from other ethnic groups seriously over-estimating my own age. We had a very pleasant evening with Kay discussing various linguistic matters. She had already made her name academically with her doctoral work on the Ijaw language, and went on to become Professor of Linguistics and Nigerian Languages in the University of Port Harcourt.

One of the teachers at the high school in Ahoada was a Mrs. Benbow, an American lady married to a Nigerian, and when she and her husband heard about us, they came to make our acquaintance. On a later occasion Mrs. Benbow returned on her own, and while she was chatting with us, a couple of young fellows were standing nearby. One of them was not from Orupata, and apparently did not know about our efforts to study Ekpeye. He made disparaging remarks about our visitor's hair style, which as it happened I heard and understood. When I responded in Ekpeye, contradicting his opinion, his face was a picture of amazement and embarrassment. Even in the most unlikely situations one should never assume that one's words cannot be understood – especially if one is a native speaker of English!

Our contacts with people from home did not cease while we were in Nigeria, but Christmas reminded us in several ways of the huge difference between what was taken for granted in England, and what was real life in Nigeria. One couple sent us a cheque "to be cashed at your nearest bank." Little did they realise that our nearest bank was 50 miles away in Port Harcourt. Eventually we were able to cash the cheque, and received the curious sum of thirty seven shillings and sixpence. An uncle of Glenys' sent us a box of biscuits, for which we had to pay almost 100% in customs duty. When we finally we got them, they were mostly in fragments. Another friend sent a nylon petticoat for Helen, together with some chocolate drops. By the time we had paid more customs duty to retrieve the parcel, the chocolate drops had melted into a gooey mess, which with the aid of our kerosene fridge we managed to solidify into one large maxi chocolate drop. But in the Nigerian climate, the nylon petticoat remained for ever unworn! We always groaned when we received notice of a parcel at the Post Office, as it meant that a demand for customs duty would inevitably follow, but we could not disappoint the well-meaning senders of the parcels by refusing to accept them.

In the New Year a young American Peace Corps worker called Gary came to live in Ahoada. We did not see a lot of him, though he would come to eat with us occasionally. When Bob heard Gary's name, he could not help dissolving into fits of sniggering, and we were not sharp enough to guess why. Eventually the penny dropped. One of the staple foods of the village was grated cassava, boiled up into a big lump from which people would take pieces to dip into a stew. This was called "gari" and sounded exactly the same as the name. The idea that anyone could have "gari" for a personal name sounded as absurd to Bob as it would sound in England for anyone to have "potato" for a personal name. As Bob put it in his own brand of English, "It is not possible that anyone answers Gari."

Through Gary we met a Canadian surveyor called Peter who was working for Shell on oil exploration in the Niger Delta. Peter was not resident in the area, but travelled here and there in a Land Rover with what seemed to us a massive amount of equipment. He would spend a night or two with us from time to time, for which he insisted on paying. The reason was that he operated on an expense account, and was expected to incur expenses up to a certain limit for food and accommodation while on field trips. If someone in his position did not report sufficient expenses, then there was a risk that the limit might be reduced, and that could cause problems for colleagues who really did need to spend what they were allowed. Faced with such logic, we had no choice but to accept his largesse. There was no lack of needy causes to disburse it on, but we had to take care to avoid mindless and insensitive generosity that would only store up trouble for the future.

Later in the year Peter was leaving the area for a few weeks, and did not want to take all his equipment with him, so he offered to leave his generator with us. We were somewhat reluctant, for several reasons. We had never handled a generator, and were a bit apprehensive about what would happen if it went wrong while in our care. Moreover we had nothing that ran on electricity, so we did not really need a generator, and having one would put a gulf between us and our neighbours. But Peter wanted to leave his generator, so in the end we agreed. It was a terribly noisy engine, and we were afraid it would upset the neighbours, but he quickly overcame such objections. The generator could only provide us with a couple of electric light bulbs, and would hardly be running to its full capacity, so Peter rigged up a few extra wires and bulbs so that some of our nearest neighbours could also have electric light as compensation for the noise. Bob, who was living with us by this time, was only too keen to be in charge of the generator, so I was relieved of that responsibility except when he went home at weekends.

So for a couple of weeks we had the unexpected and unaccustomed luxury of electric light in the evenings. The generator would run from about six o'clock till about ten. Bob would then dim the engine to give warning that it would soon be turned off, then a couple of minutes later turn it off completely. After a while we became aware that a few people who owned clocks or watches were finding that these timepieces had started to behave erratically. It transpired that they had been setting them by the generator, on the principle unknown to us that white people always turn off the lights at exactly ten o'clock. The electric light was useful while it lasted, though we were rather relieved when Peter eventually returned and took the generator away with him. The lit up neighbours had gained some prestige for a while, but nobody really felt deprived when we all reverted to our simple and trusty bat lamps. And the evenings were certainly much quieter.

Even when Peter stayed with us, we saw very little of him. His movements and his meals were very erratic, and in the evenings he would disappear into Ahoada to play bridge with Gary. Though he did not return until the small hours, he managed to be very quiet, and never disturbed us. One of Peter's attainments was blowing smoke rings, which of course Helen loved. By this time she enjoyed looking at pictures in newspapers or old copies of the Reader's Digest, and before long any photo of a man with a beard was greeted with excited cries of recognition: "Peter!"

On one occasion, an SIL colleague called Tom had come down from Enugu in the VW van to collect Joy and

Elaine from Joinkrama, and Ian and Amelia from Abua to go off to attend a workshop held on the university campus at Nsukka, north of Enugu. Before they left, we all had lunch at our house, six adults and two children, all white. Bob and Helen sat outside on the verandah watching us, and when the visitors had departed, Bob confided to us how strange he and Helen had found it to see men and women eating at the same table. So we learnt that even when we were acting in a manner completely natural to us, we could also be very foreign to our Ekpeye neighbours, and totally unaware of it.

Bob and Helen would also quietly inspect any white visitors we had and decide whether or not they were "beautiful." When they had gone we were often informed of the verdict, though not of the criteria on which it was based. Since their evaluations were frequently out of step with ours, we were at least able to grasp that Ekpeye aesthetic canons were different from western ones, though since they were never articulated, we never discovered exactly what they were. Bob and Helen were tactful enough never to tell us whether we were "beautiful" or not, and we were tactful enough not to ask!

About half way through our year in Nigeria, we made another visit to Enugu, and made the acquaintance of a couple from New Zealand, Maurice and Lorraine. Maurice was a distribution agent with the Bible Society of Nigeria, and was planning to visit our area a couple of weeks later, so Glenys asked him to bring some bacon with him, as that was a luxury unobtainable in Ahoada. The day agreed for his visit came and went with no sign of Maurice. The next day came and went, and still he did not come. We could do no more than shrug our shoulders, and we gradually forgot about the arrangement. Then one day six and a half weeks later a VW van rolled up to our house unannounced, and out stepped Maurice. And he had remembered the bacon!

Maurice went around visiting schools and churches selling scriptures in various languages, and when he left, he gave Bob ten shillings worth of booklets with single gospels that were sold for "penny penny," that is to say one penny each. Since most of them were in English, we did not expect that there would be much demand, but we underestimated Bob's entrepreneurial skill. He toted them around in Orupata and in his own village of Ekpena, and within a few days they were all gone. Maurice had hoped that Bob would use the money he received to buy more books and sell them, but Maurice was a rare visitor to the area, and as there was no practical way to order more stock, nothing came of this. But Bob enjoyed himself, and made a little extra money. It was not until after Maurice had departed that we realised we had never asked him why he was late, so in at least some ways we had adapted a little towards a more African outlook.

What effect was our totally different lifestyle having on us? Before we left England our main concern had been whether we were exposing our precious baby to unnecessary health risks by taking her to Africa. The West Coast after all had a dire reputation as "the white man's graveyard." But as so often in life the reality was less fearful than the prospect, and the risks were not as great as we might have imagined. There is no doubt that the climate was very enervating, and with the constantly broken nights, we were constantly over-tired. From time to time we were irritable with each other, or with Helen, and from time to time the slow progress on language learning and analysis was seriously discouraging, but in retrospect, the good memories far outweigh the bad. Although in later life we spent twenty years in Asia and the Pacific, our one year in Nigeria brought a much deeper involvement with an alien culture, and with living at a simple level, than we ever experienced again. In that respect, it was an excellent preparation, and gave us a very different perspective on the comforts of life that we take for granted in England. Since returning home, I have always felt slightly guilty if I cleaned my teeth under running water. Only now, forty years later, are such qualms becoming fashionable.

Helen was of course our own little European, but she adapted to life in the village with complete equanimity, adjusting to her circumstances placidly because she could not remember any others. She accepted other children and they accepted her on equal terms. Our great interest was in her language development, since this is at a peak when a child is two years old. She learnt both English and Ekpeye without hesitation or distinction. Sometimes she would say something to us in English, then turn and repeat the same thing to Bob in Ekpeye, so she clearly had some realisation that there were two different language systems in operation around her, and some perception of which language was appropriate for which people. Examples of bilingual repetition often took the form of simple commands, such as "*Kaj'eja* come," or "*Ekpe'kpo* be quiet." At other times, she would come out with sentences incorporating words from both languages, macaronic sentences as they are called, such as "Tree *da l'ehleh*" ("The tree has fallen on the ground") when she saw a very old tree with a branch that hung right down to the ground. Alicia told us that one of her boys complained to her, "Mummy, I can't understand the language that little girl speaks."

Like many West African languages, Ekpeye has a complex tonal system, and this was something that we really struggled with. Helen was uninhibited by the ingrained habits of speaking English for decades, and absorbed Ekpeye tones as effortlessly as an Ekpeye child. One day not long before we left I was walking in the village with her and we fell into conversation with a village man

I did not know. Helen joined in the conversation, and the man turned to me with a grin and delivered his verdict in pidgin: "Dis pickin de savvy our language pass you people" ("This child knows our language better than you adults"). We adults undoubtedly had a wider vocabulary than Helen did, but what he meant was that she got the tones right, whereas we made lots of mistakes. Well, it all helped to prevent us from overestimating our own ability, not that there was much danger of that.

Chapter 8
The Wildlife

Glenys and I were both brought up in a city, and although we had both spent some time on farms in childhood, we had not had much exposure to wildlife. But in a Nigerian village, wildlife is all around you, and sometimes invades the house. The first thing you notice is the noise at night. This comes mainly from two sources, the cicadas and the bullfrogs. We never saw much of the cicadas, but they must have been everywhere because we could hear them year round, with their penetrating percussion. The bullfrogs were more seasonal, and were certainly noisier in the wet season, which was when we arrived.

Nature abhors a vacuum, and the hole in the ground that we called the swamp had been colonised by various sorts of life both animal and vegetable. The vegetation thrived in decorous silence, but the bullfrogs more than made up for that. When it rained, the swamp made a convenient little reservoir for the rainwater over quite a wide area, and in very heavy rain it would fill almost to the top, though it never overflowed while we were there.

The bullfrogs of course loved it. They would honk away for hour after hour, especially in the evenings, and their competition with the cicadas sometimes made it hard for us to hear each other speak.

The swamp also made a useful rubbish dump for the neighbouring residents. This may sound repulsive, but it wasn't, because the kind of rubbish generated was almost entirely biodegradable, though we never knew that word in those days. And the rubbish was rapidly recycled by a hierarchy of scavengers. First of all children would remove anything that could conceivably be considered useful. We soon realised this and instead of throwing away empty tins we would give them to anyone who wanted them. They formed useful receptacles, especially for liquids. The most coveted items of our non-biodegradable output were the large empty tins of milk powder, which had airtight lids that were proof against ants, lizards, dogs, goats and even small children. They were so popular that we had to ration them so that the neighbours nearest us didn't corner the market. Eventually we even sold them for a penny each, with the understanding that all the pennies went in the church collection, and in the end we raised more than five shillings.

After the children came the goats. Both goats and sheep wandered freely around the village, and had to fend for themselves. Anything like pawpaw skins or banana peel would soon be gobbled up. The hens would follow and peck off any food scraps that remained. Then the lizards would move in and tackle anything they fancied that the hens had left, and finally the ants would remove anything too small for the larger scavengers to notice. This chain of privilege meant that most rubbish was gone within 48 hours of being dumped, and the swamp never became the stinking morass that we might have expected.

Sheep and goats were the main domestic animals, and we never understood how anybody knew who their owners were, since they roamed at will and never seemed to be penned up. But since one was slaughtered occasionally there must have been some kind of ownership system, though it may have been corporate rather than individual. One day soon after we arrived, our session with Reverend was unceremoniously interrupted by a noise like an army in hob-nailed boots marching over our pan roof. We all rushed outside to investigate. No, it was not children throwing stones, though this did happen occasionally, usually at the instigation of the misnamed Good, the little boy with the deformed leg. This time it was a row of vultures on the roof ridge staring balefully and hopefully at our front gate. We discovered that a goat was being butchered just outside the gate in connection with a local festival, and the vultures were hoping for a meal from the leftovers. Vultures were a lot less plentiful in Orupata than they had been in Winneba, and although they perform a useful function in the food chain, they always seemed unlovable creatures. The main avian scavengers in Orupata were the kites. We could almost always see them wheeling around over the village on the thermals, identifiable by their triangular tails. There were also hawks, fewer and smaller than the kites, and often hovering rather than wheeling. The hawks were particularly partial to chickens, and many a careless hen lost some or all of her brood to the hungry hawks. Once we witnessed the attack, and heard the pathetic cheeping of the chick as it was carried away.

Some people kept dogs, small and mangy creatures that we did not like the look of at all. One day our prejudices were justified in a spectacularly revolting way. A group of women had gathered on our verandah to take advantage of the shade, together with their babies. Suddenly one of the babies had diarrhoea, and the mother just held it out away from herself. We were not best pleased with the use of the verandah as a latrine, but before we could get a bucket of water to swill the concrete floor of the verandah, a couple of puppies appeared and before our incredulous eyes, cleared up the mess for us by eating it. None of the women seemed to find this surprising, and when the puppies had finished their snack, the mother held out the baby to have its bottom licked clean. The puppies happily obliged. The reality of life in the bush was not always idyllic, and we certainly felt no urge to own a dog after that incident.

Apart from the storeroom that was the abode of the agama lizards, our home was also shared with numerous light brown geckos, small and innocuous house-lizards. They could run up a vertical wall, or even upside down on a rafter or ceiling, and would stalk insects like a cat after a pigeon. But despite their adhesive powers, they would occasionally fall, and one evening a baby gecko landed on my foot while I was sitting reading in the kitchen. We were both rather taken aback, but after a short pause to recover his composure the gecko ran off and went about his own business, apparently unharmed. Geckos are normally rather timid, but one day I looked out of our bedroom window and noticed a female gecko digging a hole in the sand at the foot of the house wall. My head could hardly have been a yard away from her, and such a short distance would normally make a gecko run away, but this time she had more urgent business. She cocked her head on one side to keep a wary eye on me, but held her ground. As I watched she laid several eggs in the hole, and carefully covered them with warm sand before scuttling away. Whether they hatched or fell prey to some predator we never knew, but it was intriguing to see how the urge to procreate gave her an unaccustomed courage.

Geckos were a part of domestic life that we rather enjoyed, but there were other creatures that were less welcome, such as rats. After we had been in Orupata for a couple of months, the landlord had hardboard ceilings installed, the aim being to counteract the way the galvanised iron roof magnified the heat of the sun. What we had not realised was that the ceiling would provide a protected parade ground for any creatures that chose to live on it, and this included rats. As we kept all food in sealed containers, there was little to encourage them, and we seldom saw them, but we often heard them running around when we were in bed.

One evening we discovered a rat's nest behind a cupboard in the kitchen. It was made of paper, polythene bags, and incongruously a small bag of screws and a pair of Glenys' pants. We chased the occupant around the kitchen, and it eventually ran up the wall and into a corner by the ceiling. With the aid of a long stick I managed to knock it off the wall. It fell neatly through the narrow mouth of a tall yellow polythene jug whose sides sloped inwards towards the top. There was already a large grasshopper in the jug, so it had company. There was no way it could climb out up the smooth sloping plastic surface, and as the jug was half full of water, we thought that if we left it for a while it would drown. But by bedtime it was still swimming merrily around inside the jug, and we felt we would rather not leave it there overnight, just in case a rescue party somehow managed to overturn the jug. So I had the unpalatable task of accelerating its demise by holding it under the water with

117

the stick. It was surprisingly difficult to do, but the neck of the jug was narrow enough that there wasn't much other than the stick that would go through it. And in any case we did not want to use anything that would be big enough for the rat to run up and escape. Eventually its struggling ceased, and we went to bed. It was a task I was glad never to face again. Next morning both the water and the dead rat were poured down the latrine. We bought some vicious rat traps after that, and acting on local advice, baited the traps with coconut. They occasionally caught an unwary rat.

One morning Bob cried excitedly "*Ibheke*, come and see! The soldier ants are here." We came and saw, and had never seen anything like it before. A vast column of large ants, stretching into the distance and several yards wide was advancing purposefully through our front yard and towards the verandah. We did not know what their destination was. They might march straight through the house, or they might not, but if they once got in, it could be extremely difficult to get rid of them again. Our only weapon was a DDT spray that we used primarily against mosquitoes in the evenings, so we began to wield it at once. The front ranks of the ants were thrown into chaos but the message that there was opposition to their advance took a long time to reach the rear ranks, so they kept on coming. We used a lot of DDT that day, and must have killed millions of ants, but eventually the tide was stemmed and we did succeed in keeping them out of the house. The survivors turned in a different direction and left us alone. Other smaller columns appeared on later occasions, but nothing like the first one, and we did not have a recurring problem. The lizards feasted on dead ants for some time, and apparently suffered no harm from the DDT.

One day I was out walking with Helen on the other side of the swamp, when I heard some boys calling out "*Ogwo, ogwo.*" We had taken the precaution of learning this word for snake at an early stage, and I picked Helen up at once. There in front of us was a long snake moving in the same direction as we were. A neighbour very soon appeared with a large stick, and promptly dispatched the snake. The local attitude to snakes seemed to be "kill them first and then inspect them to see whether they were poisonous," and in our ignorance of snakes, we had a good deal of sympathy with this view. Not very ecologically conscious perhaps, but then ecological consciousness was not very widespread in those days, and with a small child to care for, better safe than sorry. When the snake was well and truly dead, we came closer and had a good look at it. The head was rather battered, but it did seem to have fangs, so we went home to look in our snake book to try to identify it. While Glenys and I were at the table poring over the snake book, Helen crawled unnoticed underneath the table, and suddenly touched our legs. We both yelled and jumped sky-high, and of course poor Helen had no idea what had come over us. When we recovered, we came to the conclusion that the snake had been some kind of viper, so any compunction we might have had evaporated. A few weeks later Glenys discovered a small viper in the latrine – when she was on her way out! It was quickly executed by Big Helen, and joined the rat down the latrine hole.

On other occasions much bigger snakes came to our notice. One was over four feet long, and was killed a few houses away from ours. In Ekpeye it was called *akwodu*, but we had no way of identifying it in English. We wondered if it was a black mamba, but were just glad it had not invaded our house. Another was a black snake called *ebi*, and again we could not identify it. One evening we were sitting at the table over our bedtime drinks when Glenys noticed a head waving through the slats of the verandah window shutters. It proved to be attached to a snake, which with some difficulty I knocked down and killed. After consulting our book, we decided it was probably not poisonous, but still was not a welcome visitor. The mystery was how a snake no more than three feet long could climb up the smooth surface of the wall to get through a slat that was over seven feet from the ground.

Bob arrived one morning, and announced that on his way home from Ahoada to Ekpena the previous evening,

"In the darkness I met a snake on the path, and I had to mash it." It took us a while to interpret this statement, and we had to discard theories about Bob having mashed snake for his supper. In "latingramma" "I had to mash it" meant that he had been unable to avoid treading on it because he had not seen it. An unpleasant experience, but he had not been bitten and suffered nothing worse than a fright.

Another nuisance visitor was the sand fly. Sand flies were so small that we never seemed to see them. Our "mosquito nets" were actually supposed to be sand fly nets, with a smaller mesh than that required to keep mosquitoes out. But they did not work very well. It was not until the wet season returned during our last few months in Orupata that the sandflies really became troublesome. For a few weeks we were regularly woken up by bites about four in the morning, though fortunately Helen was virtually untouched. When we had our siesta, they picked on me and left Glenys alone, so presumably my skin was tastier than hers. On one occasion she counted over sixty bites on my chest and back, whereas she had none. At least they did not carry any dreaded tropical disease, and their bites were not too itchy.

Sometimes wildlife was brought to us as potential food. One day we were offered a live squirrel, and had some difficulty persuading the young man who brought it that it was not our custom to eat squirrels. Another offering was a rodent known as a grasscutter. It was about the size of a large rabbit, with prominent front teeth. Although we knew that grasscutters were regularly eaten, we did not buy it, partly because we were not sure how to skin it and clean it, and partly because it was too big for us. Nevertheless it was interesting to see it because we had found that Grasscutter was one of the characters in the Ekpeye folk tales that we were collecting, and until this one appeared, we had no idea what they looked like. The "hero" (or sometimes anti-hero) of the folk tales was Tortoise, and a couple of times in the wet season, people showed us wild tortoises that they had caught. They too were destined for the pot.

A more distant neighbour one day called us to see a different trophy. It turned out to be a large iguana in a wickerwork trap, and apparently it was being fattened up for "chop," pidgin for food. There was quite a bit of meat on it, but somehow we were not sorry that we were not summoned to the feast when it was eventually chopped. In the wet season some children called us to the well one day to see some huge frogs that had got into it. Although the water level was by then quite high, we could see no way that the frogs would be able to escape. Some little boys were trying to shoot them with bows and arrows, presumably also for food. We did not consider that having partially disembowelled frogs in the drinking water supply was best practice, but there was nothing we could do about it. The water had to be boiled and filtered anyway, and we suffered no unpleasant consequences.

A more mysterious creature that was brought to us one day Bob declared to be a hyena, though it was much too small. It was presumably new-born, and was so small that even baby Helen could hold it in one hand. Mr. Lock, who happened to have dropped in just then, was able to identify it as a civet cat. It had pretty, spotted fur, and a ringed tail like a raccoon, and was very attractive. Happily we were not expected to eat it! The same could not be said for a weaver bird that was brought to us on another occasion. A large flock of weaver birds lived in their woven nests in some trees in a more distant part of the village. With their yellow breast feathers they were a colourful, though somewhat noisy, addition to the village population. Boys would try to catch them, and one day a successful boy brought us a terrified little yellow bird, with a bit of string tied round one leg, and the other end of the string tied to a stick. We bargained with the boy, finally bought the bird for tuppence, and promptly released it. The boy was astounded that we had wasted good money on potential meat, though in fact a weaver bird is about the size of a sparrow and would hardly make a mouthful for one person, let alone a family.

A couple of days later, a shot rang out around teatime, followed by a hubbub not far from our house. It turned out that an animal called in Ekpeye *aku* had been seen, and since it takes chickens, somebody had taken a pot shot at it, but missed. An *aku* was said to be black and about the size of a dog, but we had no idea what it was, and never heard tell of another. We thought it might be some sort of fox, though the local people did not accept this term.

Only slightly less mysterious were the *iwolo*. They had a distinctive repetitive cry, and we heard them calling from the forest frequently, especially after dark, but never set eyes on one. Some people said that they were called a tree hyrax in English, but even if this was correct, it was no help to us as we did not know what a tree hyrax was like. Our scant library did not include an encyclopaedia, and the internet was not even dreamed of in those days.

A man we did not know came to us one evening with a very young deer that he wanted to sell to us. It was about the size of a puppy, with long spindly legs that it could hardly stand on, and looked very fragile and defenceless. The man had killed the mother while hunting and wanted to make a bit more profit from the baby. Apparently he had offered it first to the Reads, but they had not made a high enough bid for his liking so he was trying his luck with us. This happened not long before we were due to leave so it was not practical for us to attempt to raise an orphan deer. We offered it some banana, which it would not take, and a saucer of milk, which it knocked over. We heard later that the hunter had eventually managed to sell it to an oil surveyor, but its chances of survival we thought were pretty low.

Smaller and less welcome creatures included cockroaches and weevils. The cockroaches would take up residence in any cardboard box, such as the ones we kept our tins of powdered milk in, but were not too much trouble. Weevils would get inside food packets, and items like flour, sultanas, or rice needed to be inspected carefully before being eaten. Glenys always sieved the rice before boiling it, and the flour before making bread, but even so, we occasionally found baked weevil in the bread. Well, to look on the positive side, it was a form of protein enrichment.

One day a group of children came to our house to show us a spider. We thought we had seen big spiders in Ghana, but this one was huge. A girl of about ten was carrying it on the back of her hand, and its body, about an inch and a half across, practically covered her hand. It was yellow and black, and nobody seemed at all scared of it, so presumably it was not poisonous. We took a photo, but did not offer to hold it in our own hands. As with so many creatures, we never saw another one like it.

On another day I was working at the language data when Bob came in and said to me "*Ida* Helen, a lamb has fallen into the well." The well was just outside our front gate, so we all went outside to look. Sure enough from inside the deep well came the pathetic baaing of the lamb as it swam around in the water. By the top of the well was the mother sheep baaing helplessly in reply to her lamb in the well. We decided we should try to get the lamb out, but how?

Across the top of the well was a tree trunk for people to stand on as they drew water with their buckets. So Bob took our bucket with a long rope, and a girl who also happened to be at the well took her bucket, then the two of them let the buckets down slowly and carefully into the well. They had to be very careful not to hit the lamb with the buckets. Meanwhile I was busy at the top of the well stopping both Baby Helen and the mother sheep from getting close and knocking Bob or the girl into the well.

They let their buckets down very gently, and dropped them under the water. Then they had to wiggle them about to try and get the lamb's front legs into one bucket and its back legs into the other bucket. The lamb did not understand what they were doing and was quite frightened. It took a long time but at last they got its front legs into one bucket and its back legs into the other bucket. Then they had to pull the two buckets up very carefully, keeping them level so that the lamb did not fall out. They had pulled the lamb about half way up when the buckets swung a bit too far apart, the lamb wriggled, and fell back down into the water.

So they had to start all over again, letting the buckets down very gently, then dropping them under the water, and catching the lamb's front legs in one bucket and his back legs in the other bucket. At last they succeeded once more, and then began to pull him up again, keeping the buckets level and close together. This time they managed to pull the lamb right to the top, and the mother sheep got so excited that I had to chase her away to stop her knocking the lamb back into the well. Glenys fetched a towel, and gently dried the very wet lamb. Then she was able to give it back to its mother. It had been badly frightened of course, but otherwise was unhurt, and none the worse for the adventure. The mother sheep was very glad to have the lamb back safe and sound, and as far as we could observe, they both lived happily ever after.

Night life, at least observable night life, consisted of moths and fireflies. The fireflies were plentiful both outside and inside the house, and we always enjoyed the cheerful flashing of their little lights in the darkness. The moths were attracted by the brightness of our pressure lamp, and were also plentiful, and in some cases huge. Although in later life we lived for many years in various tropical regions, we never again saw anything like the variety and size of the moths in Orupata. We had not been prepared for this, and were sadly ill-equipped to identify any of them, so our admiration was tempered by ignorance.

Around the village there were many species of tree, with different kinds of palm tree much in evidence, palm fruit palms, coconut palms and no doubt other varieties. It was the fruit bearing trees that impinged most on our lives, with pawpaw, banana, plantain, oranges and limes the most prominent. One man offered to sell us the entire year's crop of his orange tree, with the fruits to be picked as they ripened. We considered it, but quickly realised that with lots of little boys in the village, a sizeable proportion of the fruit would be scrumped before we got near it. So we decided it was more prudent to buy visible oranges when we needed them rather than the potential crop that we might never see. Our western urban ignorance of tropical fruit was shown up in several ways. We had never before realised that coconuts grow at the top of the trunk rather than on the branches of the trees, as they were sometimes drawn in English children's books. We had never realised that bananas grow "upside down," with the edible fruit pointing upwards rather than hanging down. Nor had we seen green oranges before, and at first needed to be convinced that they really were ripe. Probably nowadays after years of holiday travel programmes on colour television and a vastly greater range of tropical fruit in British supermarkets, such ignorance is less prevalent, but forty years ago it was not untypical. Indeed my father thought we were pulling his leg when we told him about bananas growing upside down.

Away from the house, wildlife was observable on the usually quiet cycle ride into Ahoada. The road ran through the rain forest, so there were many unfamiliar trees. The most impressive was the giant silk-cotton. Sometimes in a storm these trees would fall, and the silk-cottons seemed particularly vulnerable because their roots spread widely but not deeply. There were plenty of wild birds in the forest, of which the most noticeable were the hornbills, easily recognised because they were pictured on the one shilling Nigerian stamp in use at that time. They always looked too top-heavy to fly, but they managed to anyway.

With a whole year in the village, we were able to live through the complete cycle of the seasons. It was towards the end of the rainy season in September when we arrived, so there was plenty of water in the well, and the weather was unvaryingly hot and sweaty. Eventually the rains died away and about the end of November, the so-called cool season began, though it never seemed very cool to us. As the monsoon rains moved away southwards, the cooler air came down from the north with the harmattan wind, bringing with it dust and haze. To us it was a blessed relief, especially because it enabled us to sleep better at nights, but to our neighbours it seemed more like suffering, and for a few brief days they went around hugging themselves to keep warm. Even we used a blanket a few times at night. The harmattan was variable, and its influence was not evident every day. It hardly lasted more than a month anyway, so our respite was a brief one, and the humidity did not go down much. Even during the dry season there were occasional storms, and we relished the cool breeze that normally preceded them. From our kitchen window we could see the palm trees in the distance begin to sway, then the nearer ones, and then the wind was upon us, quickly followed by the rain. Such storms would help to raise the water level in the well, but in the dry season the roof of the house was too dirty and dusty for the water flowing off it to be worth collecting.

Because the country was so flat, there were broad skyscapes and we could see the storm clouds building up in the distance, though during the dry season they did not always bring rain to us. The well outside our compound was one of the best in the village, and more and more people used it as the dry season wore on. The water never ran out, though it did become increasingly murky and sandy with the passage of time. When the rains returned in about April, the situation quickly reverted to what we had come to regard as normal, with plenty of good water in the well. The rain storms were often accompanied by displays of thunder and lightning, all the more impressive if they occurred after dark. One night we were all awakened about four o'clock by such a storm, and we heard pathetic little cries of "Bang, bang" coming from Helen's cot. We took her into our bed for a while, but once the thunder stopped and she decided it was fun to hit me with her Teddy, she was returned to her cot.

Sunsets in Orupata were often impressive, especially if there was dust in the air, and with no light pollution, the sky at night was much clearer than in a city, with a lot more stars visible. Most impressive was the moon, which seemed bigger and brighter than we had ever known it before or since. If the sky was clear at full moon, it was so light outside that children would be out playing until quite late. Helen loved to see the moon, and saying a bilingual goodnight to "*adigwe* moon" became part of her going to bed ritual. We began to have some inkling of why the moon was treated as a goddess in ancient religions.

Chapter 9
Christmas in Abua

As Christmas drew near, we were very pleased to have an invitation from Ian and Amelia to spend a few days over the holiday with them in Abua. The first question to resolve was how we were going to get there. The amount of stuff required to keep a 21 month old daughter in the style to which she had become accustomed was surprising, and by no means negligible. Travelling to Abua on the back of a lorry, the normal local mode of transport, did not seem a practical option. Nor did 18 miles on a bicycle on an unsealed road have much appeal. We had no car and neither did our hosts, and organising one would be no simple task, as we later proved. Then we discovered that Fr. Flynn was travelling that way on the very day we wanted to go, and he readily offered to cram us and our belongings into his VW Beetle for the dusty, bumpy trip to Abua.

So in due course on 23 December he came to Orupata and collected us and we all set off. He was going to some other destination beyond Abua to visit another priest, and had goods and chattels of his own to take, so the Beetle was quite full. I was in the back seat with Helen, and Glenys, because she was smaller, shared the front seat with a crate of beer, which she managed to put on the floor under her feet. Helen and I shared the rear seat with, amongst other things, a crate of soft drinks. Fr. Flynn explained that he felt the beer was safer in the keeping of the lady. The soft drinks, he went on, were for the Protestants, and the beer for himself and his fellow priest, adding with a mischievous grin, "'Tis only us Catholic devils that drinks." As if the soft drinks were not enough to rot our Protestant teeth, he added a tin of fancy sweet biscuits to finish the job off. In all likelihood the one crate of beer would have to last the other priest quite a long time, and we certainly never saw Fr. Flynn anything other than sober.

The trip passed uneventfully, and we were soon installed in Odaga village with Ian and Amelia. Helen was very happy to make friends with their son Timothy, who was only a few weeks older than her. She particularly enjoyed Timothy's indoor swing, which was suspended from the lintel of a door. In the afternoon we had quite a long siesta to enable Helen to get used to the child's folding camp bed that we had taken with us rather than the cot she had in Orupata. After that we all went for a walk to the waterside. In this respect as in others, the Abua district was surprisingly different from Ekpeye. The villages were laid out more spaciously, and the farms were nearer the villages. There was no river as in Ahoada, but Abua was actually near enough to the sea to have several tidal creeks with salt water rather than fresh, so we had the pleasure of a quiet stroll by the landing stage.

In the evening when the children were asleep we enjoyed a leisurely chat with Ian and Amelia then turned in ourselves. Helen had no trouble with her camp bed, and never fell out of it, but it was a different story with mine. It was similar in construction to Helen's, but the metal rods that were supposed to fit into each other to form the frame kept coming out in the middle of the long side, so I was precipitated onto the concrete floor at fairly frequent intervals. Glenys was in a bed with a wooden frame, and did not suffer this indignity, but both beds were under the same mosquito net, so it was impossible for her to be undisturbed when my bed collapsed. The partition walls of the house were made of breeze blocks but to help air to circulate, they did not go right up to the roof, so Ian and Amelia were also awakened whenever I had to get up to reassemble the bed. By the end of the night I understood how Fr. Flynn felt in the scrum!

Next morning Ian proposed a walk to another village called Emilaghan, and on the way we saw for the first time a rubber plantation, with the sap being collected from the sloping incisions. The villages in Abua would have a rope stretched between two trees at the entrance, to keep out evil spirits. We never saw this in Ekpeye, but we learnt that about thirty years earlier the Abua district had suffered badly from sleeping sickness, and some villages were completely wiped out. In one place there was a juju in the form of a rather worm-eaten straw man that was supposed to keep the disease away. In the absence of adequate modern medical facilities traditional defences were deemed better than nothing!

One of Ian's tasks that day was to go out and bargain for a chicken for our Christmas dinner. When he came back with his trophy, Amelia promptly decided it was too scrawny to feed a multitude, so poor Ian had to go out again and bargain for a second chicken. Amelia normally had an Abuan girl called Ibemezi to help her in the house, but over Christmas Ibemezi decided to absent herself without consultation, so there was more work for Amelia than anticipated. Inquiries about the missing girl produced only the rather enigmatic pidgin response, "Ibemezi has disappointed," which Glenys misheard as the even more enigmatic "Mercy has disappointed."

That afternoon we went to Omelema waterside hoping for a canoe ride in the creek, but the tide was out, so we too were disappointed. We blew up some balloons for Timothy and Helen, hoping to take some photos of them, but our camera was not being co-operative, and we did not succeed. Our second night was even worse than the first, not only because of the collapsing bed, but also because of the noise from people celebrating outside the house, and from Helen inside howling whenever she was woken up. But Christmas Day was thoroughly enjoyable. Helen fell asleep at a convenient moment so we left her with Timothy and Amelia, who was preparing lunch, and went to church with Ian. The service was in a mixture of Abuan and Igbo, neither of which we understood, so it was not the most enlightening service we had ever attended. When it was over Glenys returned to help the "Mercy"-less Amelia, and Ian took me to visit an Abuan friend of his called Mr. Woodman, whose hospitality produced one bottle of orange drink and one bottle of Guinness. I suppose Ian knew what to expect, as he quickly grabbed the orange and left me the Guinness. It was my first taste of Guinness, and to this day I have taken care that it has also been the last.

Fr. Flynn was returning to Ahoada on Christmas Day, so Amelia invited him to join us for Christmas lunch. Between five adults and two toddlers we had no problem in consuming both of the chickens! But they were so adequate that we hardly had room for the Christmas pudding that followed. In the afternoon when the washing up was finally done we gave the children their Christmas presents, though inevitably Helen preferred some beads of Timothy's and he preferred her plastic train. When we went home, Helen filched Timothy's beads, while he enjoyed bursting what were left of her balloons.

Boxing Day was a Sunday, so this time Glenys and I stayed back with the children while Ian and Amelia went to church. We prepared a picnic lunch, and when they came home, we all set off again for Omelema waterside, and this time we were early enough to go out on the creek in a large canoe powered by the muscles of a friend of Ian's. We were out for four hours, travelled as far as a place called Dighiriga, and thoroughly enjoyed it. Considering the small space the children had to move around in, they were remarkably good. The term "creek" is perhaps misleading, as this waterway was often as wide as the Thames at Westminster. It was mostly lined by mangroves, trees we had never seen before. They send long, spindly roots down into the mud, so that when the water is low, they look as if they are up on stilts, an impression reinforced by the aerial roots that they drop down from their branches.

When we returned to the landing place we had started from, we discovered that of course the tide had gone out while we were on the water, so the canoe could not be brought back to the landing stage. The owner's preferred course of action was to wait till the tide came in again, but when we discovered this would not be for another four hours, we decided something else had to be done. So Ian persuaded the man to take the canoe in as far as he could, then we all got out and waded the last couple of hundred yards up the creek, knee deep in a mixture of water and mud. Ian had Timothy on his shoulders and I had Helen on mine, while Glenys and the very pregnant Amelia carried the remains of the picnic and our other odds and ends as best they could. Nobody fell over, though we were certainly a dirty and bedraggled group when we got on terra firma again. But mud can be rinsed off and clothes can be washed, so it was not long before we were back home and enjoying a good tea, with a warm glow of triumph over adversity and unco-operative nature.

Fr. Flynn had already returned to Ahoada so Bob had chartered a Ford Consul from Ahoada to bring him to fetch us next morning at 9 o'clock. At 8 o'clock a Morris Minor arrived without Bob, but with a passenger, namely the driver of the Consul. There followed a palaver in which it transpired that the Consul driver had agreed with the Morris Minor driver to substitute the smaller vehicle in order to save money, no doubt hoping for the same fare as agreed for the larger car. This was dishonest, but would have been tolerable if it were not for the fact that Ian needed to come with us to Ahoada, then make a day trip into Port Harcourt. In a Morris Minor there was not enough room for five adults plus a toddler plus baggage, so we had to insist that the uninvited passenger should not come back with us. This he was not pleased about, but in the end our demand was met, and he was left behind to make his own way back to Ahoada as best he might. We heard later through Bob that he walked the whole eighteen miles, so hopefully he learnt that cheating does not always pay. We also discovered later that we had paid the driver of the Morris Minor four shillings more than the price Bob had bargained, but that was a genuine mistake and our own faults. It was nice to be welcomed back to Orupata by an enthusiastic group of children, no doubt curious about our short absence. And it was even nicer to be back in our own comfortable bed, which did not threaten to collapse every time one turned over!

Ian managed to find public transport to Port Harcourt and back as far as Ahoada, but he was too late to reach Abua the same day, so he arrived at our home in Orupata about 8 o'clock in the evening. This enabled us to return his hospitality for the night, and he got the daily lorry back to Abua the next afternoon. The morning was of course spent discussing linguistic problems!

The Ekpeye people seemed to take about a week off to celebrate Christmas and New Year, and over the next few days we were invited to a couple of festivals. The drinking and the repetitive dancing had little appeal to us, but this was also a time for story-telling, with a group of three men and two women telling the stories. The generally noisy background made it an unsuitable environment to try to record the stories on tape, and they were told too fast for us to understand more than odd phrases, so we had to resort to recording stories spoken into a microphone in the relative peace and quiet of our own home. All these distractions meant that it took us a surprisingly long time to recover from the chaos arising from such a short absence, but we had experienced what still remains the most exotic and memorable Christmas of our lives.

Chapter 10
Plodding Along

It may have taken us a while to get back into our routine after Christmas, but at least by then we had a routine to fall back on, and there were no major changes to make in the following weeks. Our language sessions with Reverend and Bob were regular times of perceptible even if erratic and unspectacular progress. The "cool" weather made life a little easier, though not much. When the occasional storm came, as it did about once a month even in the dry season, it was a welcome event that helped to replenish the water level in the well, as well as washing the dust off the roof. Sometimes we enjoyed brilliant displays of lightning that seemed to promise rain, but then the rain disappointed us and fell elsewhere.

During the weeks following Christmas, we gained more experience of the "palaver," the traditional African way of resolving problems. Fortunately not all the disputes involved us, and all were settled fairly peaceably. The first palaver was caused by Morrison, the village cycle mechanic. For some mysterious reason he built a fence one day across the path that passed by one side of our house and led to some other houses, including that of Good's family. This did not affect us, but the people who regularly used that path were understandably annoyed, and demanded that the fence should be removed. They got no joy from Morrison, so they called in the local councillor, Mr. Ebeku. He came along to assess the situation and decided that the fence would have to go. By the end of the day it was gone, and Morrison's work was wasted. Why he wanted to have a fence there we never found out, as he did not live nearby, and it served no purpose that we could discern.

The second palaver was between Reverend and Patrick, the village carpenter. Reverend liked some of the furniture that Patrick had made for us, and asked him to make some more for him. He paid Patrick eight pounds in advance for the "stick" and the labour, but some weeks passed and there was no sign of the furniture. Reverend was very calm and patient, but persisted in trying to get what he had paid for. He began to suspect that Patrick had spent the money on something else and had not bought the materials as agreed. The situation showed no sign of resolving itself, and Reverend gradually gave up hope of receiving the furniture, and became more concerned to get his money back. Eventually he got six pounds back, and the matter was ended more or less amicably. We felt slightly guilty that it was our furniture that had given rise to the problem, but were glad that we had no plans to call on the carpenter's services again.

The third palaver did involve us. There was a padlock on the side gate that led into our back garden, for which we held one key, and Elijah's family held the other. Elijah's daughters had been in the habit of coming from time to time to cut the sugar cane that grew in the garden, and there was no problem with this. After some time, other female members of the family came to store coco yams in the kitchen at the bottom of the garden. By Ekpeye standards of politeness they should not have done this without asking our permission, but it did no harm, so we said nothing. Then one day a crowd of small boys with buckets and bowls arrived unannounced to remove a pile of sand that been sitting in our front yard, and put it in the back yard. The rationale was that then it would not be washed away. Since it had already survived at least one wet season without being washed away, and since the place they were intending to put it in was obviously too small, I did object this time. At the strategic moment, Reverend arrived and was able to call a halt to the enterprise. We went to parley with Elijah, the matter was sorted out, and the sand stayed where it had always been. It is possible that Elijah may not have been aware of everything his family did, as he did not put up much resistance to my objections.

Around this time Baby Helen went through a stage when she decided it was fun to throw food rather than eating it, and this we did our utmost to discourage. On one occasion we told her that if she did it again, she would get no dessert. She did, so she didn't! We ate our banana and custard while she stood sullenly by, watching us longingly. She knew she was being punished, and she understood why, but was too stubborn to ask for any of our food. Naturally we felt mean on the one hand, but on the other had a job not to laugh at her glowering expression. However we had to be firm and do what we had said we would. Fortunately this particular form of behaviour did not last long. Pushing the boundaries is an inevitable stage of development, and may seem to be fun, but not at the cost of banana and custard!

We all took malaria prophylactic pills called Paludrine every day. Baby's pill was only a quarter of one of ours, and was usually concealed inside a piece of toast and covered in Marmite. She was aware of this, and seemed to think it was a necessary part of the routine. Occasionally she would ask for and be given one of the saccharine tablets that Glenys used, and that too would have to be hidden in toast and covered in Marmite. If Helen had a tummy upset, she would be given some kaolin, and this she really liked. There would be cries of "More, more," which turned to howls of disappointment when the bottle was put away. On the other hand, if Helen ran a temperature,

Glenys would administer a dose of Malarex, which was quite bitter and unpleasant to the taste. To prevent Helen from spitting it out, one of us would hold her nose while the other one put the spoon in her mouth, so that she had to swallow the medicine in order to take the next breath. Strangely she rather enjoyed this procedure, and seemed to imagine that having one's nose held while taking medicine was somehow part of the therapy. Eventually even a dose of kaolin was accompanied by a request to "hold my nose."

Helen was talking quite a lot by this stage, and it was a challenge to try to record some of her utterances to send home for her grandparents to enjoy. But as often with small children, however voluble they may be in normal circumstances, the sight of a microphone reduces them to silence, and recording was no easy task. We did get some results, but probably never really did her justice.

Life in the village proceeded at its own leisurely pace, interspersed with both tragedy and comedy. One man, the father of two young children, fell out of a palm tree he had climbed to cut the fruit, and was killed. He was not someone we knew, and we heard of the mishap only when the funeral took place. The precarious side of life was accepted more phlegmatically in the village than it would have been in England.

On another occasion, our day was brightened by a chorus of delighted little voices chanting in our front yard. The chant, repeated several times, went like this:

"Ibheke kpo budha,
akalomu kpoloshia.
Biiii!"

We did not understand it, though it appeared to be directed at us, and at me in particular. When I went out to talk to the children, their faces radiated good-natured mischief, but they ran away, so we asked Bob to explain what was going on. Not without some embarrassment he told us that the chant meant something like "When the white man takes his snuff, then the snot runs down his nose." The *"Biii!"* at the end was an onomatopoeic representation of a sneeze, the Ekpeye equivalent of "Atishoo." Apparently the children had at some time heard me sneeze, and this little rhyme was the result. Since there had never been any Europeans living in the village before, the sound of a European sneeze could hardly have been a regular occurrence, so we assume the chant was made up for the occasion rather than being a traditional children's rhyme. We heard it a number of times as the days passed, and it did not always need a sneeze to provoke it. Since I had never taken snuff or used any kind of tobacco, we were not sure how it could have arisen, but the children enjoyed it, especially if they thought I might give chase to them. I hardly needed to open the gate of the verandah before they rushed off with ecstatic screams of mock terror and disappeared through neighbouring doorways, to peep out from behind the legs of some compliant adult, giggling in convenient safety. Needless to say Baby Helen quickly learnt the chant, and it has now been passed on to our granddaughter!

As time went on, the bicycle spent fewer and fewer nights with us. On weekdays, Bob usually rode it to his home in Ekpena, and back again next morning, so it was available if either of us needed to go into Ahoada during the day. Big Helen would use it to go to market in Ahoada when there was shopping to be done, and on Saturday afternoons she was allowed to ride it back to Obholobholo, bringing it back on Monday mornings. This system worked fairly well, though there was occasionally a squabble between Bob and Helen over who had priority. This problem was ended in a way we would not have chosen. One day Bob announced that he had been able to get a job with one of the companies that was prospecting for oil in the Niger Delta region. It was not very clear what he would be expected to do, but it was a privilege for a lad of his age to be offered any kind of job, and even if we had had the means of preventing him from taking the opportunity, it would not have been fair to do so. It would give him some experience outside his home area, and almost certainly more money than we could pay him, so after a delay of a couple of weeks, we bade him a reluctant farewell. We were in any case planning a few weeks out of the village shortly.

Village life may have pursued its regular and unhurried course, but the same could not be said for the wider political situation in Africa. In November 1965 the white supremacist regime of Ian Smith in Rhodesia had made a Unilateral Declaration of Independence from Britain, UDI. Having no radio, we learnt about this belatedly from the Guardian Weekly. If the Guardian Weekly, or rather its reports of the reactions of the leaders of other African countries, were to be believed, the whole of Africa was highly indignant about the UDI. I was curious to know the opinions of the people of Orupata, and went round asking them. I soon gave up, however, as I could not find a single person who had ever heard of Rhodesia, let alone held opinions about it. But then, the Beatles were at the height of their fame at this time, yet Big Helen had never heard of them! I wrote to the editor of the Guardian Weekly to apprise him of both these facts, but it seemed that such information did not suit his view of the world, and the letter was never published.

But trouble was in store nearer to home, and in January 1966, there was a military coup in Nigeria in which the federal government of the northern leader Alhaji Sir Abubakar Tafawa Balewa was overthrown. He and the premiers of the Northern and Western Regions, Alhaji Sir Ahmadu Bello and Chief Samuel Ladoke Akintola were all killed. The government was taken over by General Johnson Ironsi, an Igbo from the Eastern Region. As before, we knew nothing of all this at the time and only picked up second hand pieces of information from various people as the days went by. One day I called on Fr. Flynn, who gave me an account of events so graphic that I could have been forgiven for imagining that he had witnessed them himself.

"Have you heard the news?" he cried excitedly. Before I could even answer he went on, allegro and staccato, like a typewriter with no punctuation keys, "There's-been-a-revolution-and-the-miltary's-taken-over-the-country-and-Ahmadu-Bello's-dead-and-when-I-heard-it-I-thought-thank-God-for-that-but-I'm-sorry-for-his-poor-wife." At last he paused for breath. "Or should I say his poor wives?" I had no knowledge of the matrimonial arrangements of the late politician, and so was unable to answer this question.

Despite Fr. Flynn's animated account, life in the Niger Delta continued as if nothing had happened. Since General Ironsi was from the east, it seemed unlikely that there would be any major changes there, and indeed there were not, though a short while later I did receive a rather anxious letter from my supervisor at SOAS asking whether we were all right. In fact political activity in high places aroused little interest in remote villages where people felt themselves to be far distant from the levers of power. Most people probably wanted nothing more than to be left in peace to continue their time-honoured agricultural round. Nobody in Orupata could foresee the suffering that the next few years would bring.

Among the gifts we had received at Christmas was a small tape of some music recorded in the church in Bristol where Glenys had been brought up. Among the pieces on it was a musical setting of the words of Isaiah 26.3 in the King James Version, "Thou wilt keep him in perfect peace, whose mind is stayed on thee" sung by some friends. We had enjoyed the tape anyway, but in a time of political uncertainty, the words became both an encouragement and a challenge to us.

Arrangements were in hand for SIL to hold a major linguistic workshop at the University of Nigeria campus at Nsukka, north of Enugu. We were invited to attend, but felt that with the limited experience of Ekpeye that we had behind us, and the limited time of study left ahead of us, we should not go for the whole three month period of the workshop. It was being led by Prof. Kenneth L. Pike from the University of Michigan, one of the leading experts in the world at linguistic analysis, so we did not want to miss completely the opportunity of getting some help from such an eminent scholar. So we decided that we would compromise, and attend just the middle part of the workshop. Our colleagues Ian and Amelia from Abua, and Elaine from Engenni both had considerably longer fieldwork behind them than we did, so they were more advanced with their language analysis, and were going for the whole workshop. Amelia was soon to deliver another baby, and Nsukka was a much more convenient place for the delivery than Abua.

So on the appropriate day, another SIL member called Tom drove the VW van down from Enugu to collect them all. Our home was a convenient assembly point, and after having breakfast with us, Tom went to Mbiama to collect Elaine off the boat from Joinkrama, and took Glenys with him, as she had never been down there before. When they got back to Orupata, Elaine stayed with us to discuss linguistic problems while Tom went over to Abua to fetch Ian, Amelia and Timothy. They brought with them Timothy's swing that Helen had enjoyed so much at Christmas, as he would have no need of it for several weeks. Helen was pleased to see Timothy again, but even more pleased to see the swing, which was now hung from her own bedroom door. After lunch, all our guests left for Enugu, and relative peace descended on us again, though our appetites had been whetted for the workshop that was yet to come.

Some days later on the occasion of another funeral in the village, a group of half a dozen women we did not know presented themselves at our house asking to hear us speak Ekpeye. We chatted with them for a while, and then they went away again. After they had gone, Big

Helen informed us rather disapprovingly that they were all "harlots" in Ahoada. To us they did not appear different from any other Ekpeye women of our acquaintance, but Helen probably knew what she was talking about. At the time of a funeral, they had presumably come to pay their respects to the dead rather than to ply their trade. We were never aware of any prostitution in Orupata, though if there was any, it seems unlikely that anyone would have drawn our attention to it.

Helen was an intelligent girl, and one evening over the washing up, she started asking us questions about the Bible. But the questions, involving geography, history and culture, were quite different from those an English teenager might have asked. For instance, "Is Jerusalem in heaven?" We could only guess how such an idea might have arisen – perhaps from some village preacher's misunderstanding of the picture of the heavenly Jerusalem in Revelation 21. But a belief in the everyday interaction of the physical and the spiritual is widespread in Africa, so maybe the question should not have seemed so strange to us as it did.

"Were Abraham, Isaac and Jacob real people?" This is a question that exercises western academics, though Helen would not have been aware of that. So far as we were concerned, it was impossible to imagine that people whose characters are depicted so vividly in the book of Genesis could have been anything other than real.

"Was Jesus English?" Indeed he was not, but what had made her think he might have been? Missionaries may sometimes present a Jesus dressed in the cultural trappings of their own society, but all the missionaries Helen would have come across were Americans, and we could not imagine that they would ever have given the impression that Jesus was English! Hopefully our answers gave her some helpful information, but on the other hand, maybe we learnt more from her questions than she did. We at least gained a better understanding of what it must be like to be Christian without having access to the Bible in your own language, and certainly we saw afresh the importance of translating the Bible into languages that people could really understand.

Chapter 11
Interlude on the Move

When the time came for us to go to Nsukka near the end of February, the first problem was how to get there. The SIL minibus was not available, so we had to make our own arrangements. It turned out that the most convenient way was by train from Port Harcourt to Enugu. But that still left the problem of how to get to Port Harcourt, and this was where the expatriate community proved extremely helpful. Alicia lent us a suitcase that was more portable than the trunks and boxes that our goods were stored in, and Samuel and Bernice at the Adventist Hospital discovered that they needed to go to Port Harcourt on the same day as we did, so they offered us a lift. In fact they not only offered us a lift, but invited us to spend the previous night at their home on the hospital compound so that we could all make an early start. Alicia took us out there, and it was a pleasant change for us to be in a house that, unlike ours, was not still half built. Helen accepted the change of situation with equanimity and settled happily to sleep. After the evening meal we persuaded Samuel to play some pieces on his piano. It was a rare treat, and we had a strange sense of unreality as the melody of "Jesu, joy of man's desiring" floated out through the windows into the surrounding jungle. The tape we made of Samuel's rendering gave us pleasure on many a subsequent evening.

The planned early start did not materialise because next morning Samuel had to appear at the courthouse in Ahoada as a medical witness in a manslaughter case. This arose from a shooting incident that had taken place during a hunting expedition in the bush, an event of which we had previously heard nothing. Our departure was not long delayed, however, and we were delivered at Port Harcourt railway station safely and punctually for the train. For the first time in our lives we were travelling first class, largely for convenience with Helen, and we were honoured by being escorted to our private compartment by no less than the stationmaster himself. We travelled in unwonted splendour as the compartment had bunks and a private toilet and washbasin, though the water supply ran out before the journey was over. Much of the route northwards via Aba and Umuahia lay through the rain forest, so the scenery was rather monotonous. We were surprised at the width of the space cleared of trees on either side of the track before the forest began, but then we realised that it was necessary to allow enough space for any dead trees to fall without blocking the track.

We had a couple of nights in Enugu, and that gave the opportunity to do some shopping. It also gave me my first experience of driving the SIL Land Rover around the town, not something I enjoyed, though the vehicle finished the trip with no more bumps or scratches than it had started with. One of our tasks was to collect from the Post Office a parcel containing no less than 7lbs of sweets that friends in England had kindly sent us. For this we had to pay one pound fourteen shillings and eight pence in customs duty, vastly more than we would ever have spent on sweets ourselves. Some of the sweets had gone soft but they were still edible, and as we were going to be in a community with several expatriate children in it, none of them were wasted.

It was some relief that the VW van was available for the journey on to the university campus at Nsukka. Some of the other workshop participants were passing through Enugu after hospital appointments further south in Umuahia, so we all travelled up to Nsukka together. The country north of Enugu was more interesting, with undulating low hills and a more open savannah terrain. The accommodation on the campus seemed unbelievably luxurious, with our own private shower and bathroom with all mod con. Best of all, the climate was much more to our liking, with a considerably lower humidity than the Niger Delta, so that although the day time temperatures were actually higher, they felt more comfortable. Helen slept far better too, so we had a lot more energy for the work that we had come to do. The dining room and study rooms were air-conditioned and that increased the incentive to spend as much time as possible working. Perhaps the most welcome luxury was an open-air swimming pool, which we made use of as often as possible.

There were quite a few small children at the workshop, and there was a crèche for them on working days. Helen settled happily in the crèche, where she already knew Timothy, and they were soon to be seen going round hand in hand, looking more like teenagers than two-year olds. Timothy now had a baby sister by the name of Alison Ruth. To Amelia's chagrin, Helen took more interest in the new arrival than Timothy did, and called her by name some time before her big brother deigned to do so.

Although we had had occasional linguistic discussions in Orupata with Elaine and with Ian, neither Engenni nor Abuan, the languages they were learning, was related to Ekpeye, so the problems of analysis that they faced were often very different from ours. At Nsukka we were also able to talk with Paul and Inge, a Swiss couple, who though they lived a long way from us, were working on a language called Izi that did belong to the same language family as Ekpeye. They had been in Nigeria longer than we had, so they were further ahead with their language study, and the problems they faced were much more likely to be relevant to us. Paul and Inge had a little boy about Helen's age called Bernhardt, who could speak some Izi, and as it was related to Ekpeye, some degree of communication between him and Helen was possible, though to our observation, it consisted mainly of Helen saying "Don't" in Ekpeye, and Bernhardt ignoring her.

The workshop was an opportunity for teams studying different languages to stand back from their daily grind and take a more detached view of the data they had collected. Different people gave descriptions of various problems they faced, and where possible they presented the solutions that they favoured. The rest of the time was spent either working on one's own data, discussing problems with colleagues who were working on related languages, or having consultation sessions with the guest leader of the workshop, Prof. Kenneth Pike from the University of Michigan. The problems uppermost in our minds were how to analyse the tone system of Ekpeye, and how to describe the way the many verbal suffixes functioned, and these were what we hoped Prof. Pike would be able to help us with. But in our first session with him, he did not look at any of our language data, but rather spent the time trying to get to know us a bit, to stretch our minds and broaden our horizons. My sights were firmly set on completing my doctoral studies, which seemed an elusive enough goal at that stage. His advice however was not to worry about that, but rather to look ahead to the first three academic papers I would publish when the doctorate was finished. No such ambition had ever entered my head, and my mouth probably dropped wide open. Tunnel vision is often a problem for doctoral students, and I was no exception. But not surprisingly, he was right, and eventually after the thesis was finished, I did publish four technical articles on Ekpeye. As far as I have been able to trace, they are still the only academic publications on this language.

During our spell at Nsukka, Helen had her second birthday. There were several birthday cards for her, but with the perversity that comes so naturally to children, she enjoyed the envelopes at least as much as the cards. And the little lorry we had brought with us for her to push along was soon pushed over the verandah – fortunately with no damage to anyone else, though it lived the rest of its life with a bent back axle. On Helen's first birthday in Enfield we had taken a photo of her with snow on the ground. As it happened her second birthday fell on a Saturday so we were free to spend a good deal of it at the open-air swimming pool. The contrast could hardly have been more pronounced.

Another new cultural experience for Helen at Nsukka was the flush toilet. She loved pulling the flush, so we had to restrict her to pulling it when she had earned the right to do so by using the toilet for its intended purpose. We did not make rapid progress! The supply of water was limited, and it was not to be wasted by pulling the flush unnecessarily. One day the water was off most of the day, and I eventually had to sneak out under cover of darkness and filch a bucketful for us to wash in from an ornamental pond.

Our ten days at the workshop flew by, and although we did not arrive at spectacular solutions to our problems of language analysis, the time spent was profitable enough that we decided to spend a bit longer there than originally planned. But first we had another excursion to enjoy. For some years we had been friends with Hugh and Vi, missionaries in a village called Ika, not far over the border into what was then the Northern Region of Nigeria, and they had invited us to visit them. They were coming down to Nsukka the following weekend, and offered to collect us to return with them to Ika. They had various jobs to do in Nsukka, including giving their four boys a chance to swim in the pool, so it was after 9 p.m. when we finally left, and past midnight before we arrived at Ika. The journey was only about 80 miles, but most of it was on unsealed roads, so progress was slow, and over the last 16 miles, pretty bumpy in a vehicle carrying four adults and five children. It was our first experience on the dusty laterite roads common in that area, and we had not realised how easily the red dust raised by vehicles penetrates everywhere. By the time we arrived in Ika, we were all red-faced and had red dust in our hair, ears and noses, so even at that late hour a shower was needed before we could decently go to bed.

Ika seemed to be in the middle of nowhere, but due to its proximity to three different language areas, it had become quite a centre for mission work. The location was not far enough north to be in the predominantly Muslim area, and the surrounding communities had followed traditional African religions. The senior missionary, Mr. Dibble from the USA, had first arrived there in 1921, and was still there. He had busied himself with Bible translation as a high priority, and when he was obliged to move out of the area during the Second World War, he left in the hands of the small group of local Christians about half a dozen typewritten copies of his work. When he returned after the war, he was astounded to find that during his absence, the local Christians had used the translation to such effect in spreading the good news that the church had multiplied beyond his dreams. The few copies of the translation that survived were dog-eared with use, and bore eloquent testimony to the importance of new churches having access to scripture in their own language.

In due course, Mr. Dibble had been joined by other missionaries, both American and British. These included two of his own sons (who had grown up as native speakers of the local languages) and their families, and by four other families as well as by several single missionaries.

The facilities developed at Ika over the years included a maternity hospital, a printing shop, and a short-term Bible school for local Christians. Under Mr. Dibble's leadership the whole Bible had been translated into Igala, the language of the immediate vicinity, and a good deal of the New Testament had been drafted in Agatu. A start had been made also in another language called Eloyi. These latter two projects were the responsibility of our friends Hugh and Vi respectively, so we were still in the company of people with a lively interest in analysing languages.

Ika was remote enough that foreign visitors were not frequent, and we were made very welcome, enjoying meals in all the different homes during our nine-day stay. It seemed that the fatted calf was killed everywhere we went, and we felt quite bloated by the end of the week. One of the blessings that we received at Ika was a recipe for making ice cream, and after we got home ice cream appeared more or less regularly on our menu. Not up to home standards perhaps, but nevertheless a welcome addition to our diet. We were shown around the printing shop where the press was powered by a truly sustainable source, a man on a bicycle whose wheels had been removed! We also toured the hospital, where Glenys spent quite a bit of her spare time. After gaining her medical qualification, she had done a diploma in obstetrics and retained her interest in this branch of medicine. She even assisted Eustace, the missionary doctor, in performing a caesarean section.

Helen had been born in University College Hospital in London, in those days one of the relatively few hospitals in Britain where fathers were allowed to be present at the birth. But because of complications, Glenys herself had to have a caesarean section, and so I lost the opportunity to be present, one of the bigger disappointments of life. Here at Ika I was allowed to witness a normal delivery, and although I had no emotional involvement, it was still a privilege to see the arrival of a new baby girl, and I remain grateful to that unknown Nigerian mother for permitting this. The baby took a couple of minutes to start breathing properly, but in the end all was well.

The days at Ika were not all holiday, and I had some time free to continue working on Ekpeye most days. And I could not resist helping Hugh and Vi's boys in making up a plastic railway engine kit that they had acquired from somewhere or other. Glenys and I also explored the area within walking distance, which in the heat was not very far, but we did climb up a nearby hill early one morning to gain a view over the surrounding savannah. We were surprised that from the top we could see no sign of human habitation anywhere except in Ika itself. Villages were evidently further apart here than in the Niger Delta. The area where the homes of the missionaries were located was quite spread out, and they had taken care to make it attractive with plants like bougainvillea, hibiscus, frangipanni and pride of Barbados that we saw little or nothing of in the delta. There seemed to be far fewer lizards than in Orupata, but we did see some tiny beautiful blue kingfishers, and a gigantic moth with a wingspan of about eight inches.

Helen enjoyed being with other children, and we learnt something of the problems of education for missionary families in remote areas. At Ika there were no less than 18 missionary children aged from under one year up to about 14, and one of the missionary ladies was their teacher. It was a huge challenge to teach children aged from five to fourteen in one class. Although there were good American postal courses available, they were not always compatible with the British system. The American families held strong views about not separating children from their parents by sending them home to school for secondary education. There are obvious advantages to keeping a family together, but we could not help noticing that the older American children, while very much at home with their Nigerian peer group, seemed to have little interest in the world outside Nigeria. They found it hard to converse with us, and we wondered how difficult it would be for them to adjust when they eventually had to return to America for tertiary education. What to do about secondary education for Helen was a question that we ourselves were to face a decade later, and the decision was among the most difficult we ever had to make.

On our second Sunday, Hugh took me to a place about a dozen miles away where there was a convention for young Christian men. We arrived in time for an open-air communion service that took place under the shade of a mango tree. Neither bread nor wine were indigenous or locally available, so the elements of the communion were water and a beancake that was so peppery it gave me quite a shock. But these were the staples of daily life in the area and probably conveyed the significance of the communion more pertinently than alien bread and wine would have done. As a visitor I was expected to speak, and this brought a new experience of having my words interpreted. Interpretation took place from English into Igala and from Igala into Agatu. Each speaker seemed to take longer than the last, and I began to wonder how much the end product resembled what I had actually said. Since I knew nothing of either language, I had no way of checking. The other problem was that the time lapse between my utterances was so long that I had difficulty remembering what I had already said or had intended to say next. Since then I have spoken with an interpreter many times, but never into more than one language, so this still remains the most difficult interpretation experience I have ever had.

During our last couple of days at Ika Helen developed a painful urinary infection, though the tests available there showed no conclusive results. When we left, we had the offer of a ride back to Enugu with two of the missionaries who needed to go there, and were glad to accept. Helen howled for much of the way back to Enugu, which did not make the journey any easier for the driver, but we were relieved to be able to take her somewhere where there were more extensive medical facilities. We also planned to do our shopping to stock up on stores for our second six months in the village. However the larger stores were low on stocks because it was near the end of March, that is, the end of the financial year, so we could not get everything we had expected to.

The railway line in Enugu ran not far from the SIL house where we were staying, and it was at this time that Helen began to take an interest in the trains. There were many coal trains puffing slowly and noisily up an embankment, so one could not be unaware of them. Her interest peaked one evening when she was asleep, but nevertheless stood up to call out "Bye-bye train." It was during those few days in Enugu that we made the acquaintance of the local distribution agent of the Nigerian Bible Society, a New Zealander called Maurice. Neither of us knew it then, but our paths were to cross again later many times in many different places. Maurice was planning a visit to our area shortly, so we offered him accommodation. Since he would be coming direct from Enugu, Glenys asked him to bring some bacon, which was unobtainable in Ahoada. Although he came six weeks late, he didn't forget the bacon.

We were able to get more medical tests done on Helen in Enugu, and to obtain some medicine that Glenys hoped would do the trick for her. While we were there, I had a scary experience. I was opening a bathroom door, and paused to speak to Glenys, with my hand around the edge of the door. Suddenly something out of sight bit my finger. I yelped, more with shock than pain. Clearly I had to find out what had bitten me, so I peeped very gingerly round the door, not knowing whether to expect a snake or a spider or …. The result was something of an anti-climax, as the perpetrator was only a praying mantis, disappointed to find that a human finger was not the answer to its prayers. I was relieved that it was nothing noxious, and peaceful co-existence was resumed. Eventually we were able to take a Peugeot 404 taxi back to Nsukka for another week's work there. The driver seemed to treat it a matter of pride to stay in the highest possible gear on hills for as long as possible, so frequently the engine was labouring to the point of stalling, and all for no purpose that we could discern.

The final week in Nsukka passed quickly with the same mixture of discussion, consultation, analysis and library reading. On our last day we were busy packing and did not have time to go to the pool, though we took Helen for a quick paddle. Prof. Pike was in the pool, and happily took her on his back for more of a swim than we could give her that day. This kind of spontaneous human touch is something that goes a long way to cement solidarity in any organisation, and is an essential element in leadership that is often lost sight of in today's world, obsessed as it is by management techniques that demote people to mere "human resources."

On the first of April we went down from Nsukka to Enugu in the SIL Land Rover. Since we had done all that we could in Enugu, there was no point in spending any more time there, so we made the rest of the journey back to Orupata the same day. For this we had the new SIL Peugeot 404, which was a dream to drive after the Land Rover. An SIL member called Paul came down with us and took the 404 back to Enugu the same day. We had many things to do by way of sorting goods and chattels and reorganising ourselves for village life, and could not even manage to eat a proper meal that evening. While we were busy, a group of children came to our verandah and said "*Ida* Helen, *Ina* Anti calls you." I could not think of any reason why Mother-of-Anti should call me, but I walked across the few yards to her house, only for her to assure me with an enigmatic smile that she had not called me. The children were delighted and my short walk back to our house was accompanied by triumphant cries of "*Effelifooloo, effelifooloo*." This did not carry any meaning in Ekpeye that I could make out. A couple of hours later the penny dropped, and I remembered the date. This was the nearest the children could get to saying "April fool."

Chapter 12
Alarms and Excursions

One of the pieces of news that awaited us in Orupata
was of the political and military excitements that had taken
place in our absence, of which we had heard nothing. It
seemed that an aspiring politician called Boro had led an
armed gang around terrorising some of the areas deeper
into the Niger Delta, to the west of the Orashi River, as part
of an attempt to set up an independent state in the Niger
Delta. He had never got anywhere near Orupata, though
people had been afraid that he might come. Eventually
a contingent of the Nigerian army had been sent to the
area, and they had roared through Orupata in their trucks
on their way to Mbiama. We never discovered exactly
what had happened, but anyway, the army had sorted the
matter out, the rebellion was put down, and Boro himself
was captured and condemned to death for treason. The
sentence was commuted and he was later released. He
was eventually killed in the Biafran war, fighting, perhaps
rather unexpectedly, on the Federal Government side. The
building of the road to Yenagoa had been temporarily
suspended, and for a while Roy had to spend his days

playing cards with his workmates instead of getting on with the job. On the whole, this was a type of excitement that we were not sorry to have missed.

Happier news for us was that Bob was home again for his Easter break. His work with the oil company was hard, the conditions uncongenial, and his mother did not want him to go back, so we lived in hope that he would decide not to. Big Helen meanwhile became increasingly erratic in her performance, and we were wondering whether we should dispense with her services. In particular she had been taking longer and longer over her trips to Ahoada market, and coming up with increasingly unconvincing reasons for this. One day she justified her lateness with the statement "I saw a cripple in the market, and I had to stop and mock him." The first part of the statement may well have been true, though I had never seen such a person in the market myself. But the second part, whether true or not, showed a huge gap between her expectations and ours. Our immediate reaction was one of revulsion towards such an attitude. But from the casual way in which she made the statement, we wondered on later reflection whether there was more to this than met the eye. It was hard to imagine that Helen herself would have initiated public mockery of another human being who had presumably done nothing to deserve it. Had she rather joined in something that was already going on? Could it be that in Ekpeye society people with physical deformities played some recognised role in making themselves the butt of jokes that were perhaps intended to deflect such misfortunes from others? Was this some kind of traditional protective ritual that might even have given the crippled person some status in society, perhaps reminiscent of the role of court fools in medieval Europe? By the time we had thought about it, the incident was long past, and we never reached any clearer understanding of what had been going on.

One reason for Helen's slackness was that she was involved in some kind of marriage palaver. The father of a young man she was friendly with alleged that he had paid £40 as a bride price for her to marry his son, but she had not been handed over. Helen's father claimed that the sum paid was only £5, and that it was for something else. Reverend had been a witness to the transaction, so it seemed likely that the young man's father was lying. Helen herself did not seem to care whether she married the young man or not, though this may have been just a front. We never learnt the final outcome of the dispute, though we did hear later on the grapevine that Helen was to marry a policeman in Lagos. Whether she actually did we never discovered. Anyway Helen decided to stop working for us at the end of April, and we accepted her departure with some relief as this absolved us from the unpleasantness of firing her. Another reason (or excuse) for her to leave was that her mother was "seriously ill."

Mother had apparently been to the hospital at Joinkrama for a few days, but the only thing approaching a diagnosis that we ever heard was "She get trouble for belly." Since this could cover anything from indigestion to cancer, it was impossible to tell what the trouble was.

One of the less fortunate things that Helen did during her final week with us was to upset a blancmange that Glenys had made and put on top of the kerosene fridge to set. The gooey mess ran down the back of the fridge and into the works, where it began to coagulate around the fins. There was not much space between the fins, and they were accessible only to a long screwdriver, so I spent over an hour trying to scrape out the blancmange with the screwdriver. Overall I was moderately successful, and the fridge still worked. But picking up blancmange with a screwdriver is not a pastime to be recommended, and will never feature as an Olympic sport.

In the end Bob did not return to his job, so was free to start working with us again. We invited him to take over Big Helen's role as well, so he came to live with us. He was not the quietest mortal we had ever met, but he was a cheerful and reliable worker, and we enjoyed having him around. He had relatives in Orupata, so he was not completely separated from his own family, and was able to go home at weekends as Helen had. Baby Helen already knew and liked him and did not have to get used to someone else, so the new arrangement suited everybody, and lasted until our departure.

The rains had begun just as we returned to Orupata, so the well filled up again, and we were once more able to supplement our water supply by collecting the rain water from the roof. The hen, which Reverend had kindly looked after for us while we were away, was returned to our care. She seemed to attract numerous suitors, so we lived in hope of a supply of free eggs in due course. Reverend had begun translating the Gospel of Mark into Ekpeye in preparation for a course on translation that he was to attend in Enugu, and I was able to spend some time with him going over part of it. The Ekpeye script had not been officially settled, so the translation was typed up in three different spelling systems. This enabled us to test it on different people in order to see not just how well they could understand the translation, but also how well they could read the different scripts.

On the red side of the ledger, we were regularly having trouble with the pressure lamp that was our main source of light after sunset, and the fridge was becoming temperamental even before the blancmange episode, and it took time to sort out both these problems. The return to the very humid climate meant that Helen began to give us bad nights again. We managed to devise a way of keeping the windows of her room open at night to provide a little more breeze, but it did not make much difference. Among our baggage we discovered a small doll with eyes that closed when she was tipped backwards, and this proved very popular with Helen, and a source of sheer wonder to the village children. Inevitably the doll was called Alison Ruth ("Woof") after Timothy's new sister.

Glenys' birthday came in April, so we wanted to celebrate a little. There was no restaurant to go to, so our celebrations consisted of opening a tin of ham and a tin of new potatoes. This may not seem much, but both items were extravagances in Orupata. A few days later we had celebrations of a very different sort. The aged father of Duke (Duke of Edinburgh, that is!) died and was given funeral rites of great pomp and ceremony as befitted someone who had apparently in his prime been a renowned warrior. Just what this meant was never explained, but the funeral celebrations lasted several days and were accompanied by the expenditure of a good deal of ammunition. On the last day, the ceremony included the decapitation of a dog. We could have gone along to witness this, but decided that it was something we could spare ourselves without giving offence. For Bob, however, this was an unusual and intriguing procedure, and not to be missed. We had no objection to his attendance, but he returned bursting with gory details while we were having lunch, so we had to put an embargo on his account until our meal had gone down.

In the evening of that same day, the finale of the funeral involved more shooting, this time from what people referred to as a "cannon." We never saw the weapon, though during the evening we did hear an exceptionally loud bang. A few minutes later people came running to tell us that a man was dead. They clearly expected us to do something about it, so although we did not normally go far after dark, we felt that on this occasion we should make an exception. Glenys grabbed our first aid box and ran off to the village. I gathered Baby Helen up, locked the house and followed at a more leisurely pace. The nearer Glenys got to the scene of the tragedy, the less serious it became. First the man concerned was not dead, but was badly wounded. Then he was slightly wounded. When Glenys arrived, she found him sitting up with a broad grin on his face.

Helen and I were not sure where the man was to be found, but it was not difficult to locate him, as there was a noisy and excited crowd around the doorway of one house in the main part of the village. When I pushed my way through and gained entry, there was Glenys putting antiseptic cream on the arms and chest of a man with extensive powder burns and a small flesh wound on one forearm. I put Baby down, and she picked her way to the front through a forest of adult legs. There she peered up at Glenys, and said "Hello Mummy" with great aplomb as if this were an everyday occurrence.

Presumably the "cannon" had backfired somehow. The "corpse," Godwin by name, was alive enough to walk back to our house with us to get some codeines to take as painkillers. Glenys told him that he should go next day without fail to the Adventist Hospital to get an anti-tetanus injection. When she checked up on him, it was to learn that he had felt much better in the morning, and so instead of visiting the hospital he had gone climbing palm trees to tap the fluid to make palm wine. He survived anyway, apparently none the worse for his premature "death."

A few days later Ian and Amelia returned from Enugu in the SIL VW van, and kindly delivered to us the stores we had not been able to get when we had been there. John, the branch director, took advantage of their journey to visit all three of the teams in the Delta area, and stayed one night with each team, the first night with us. Next morning, he suggested that he and I should go and visit the District Officer, the senior government representative in the Ekpeye area. John was surprised that I had not already done so, but I had not been aware that I ought to have. In England one would not dream of dropping in on the local mayor when moving to a new town, so it had simply not occurred to me to take the equivalent course of action in Nigeria. I was a little apprehensive about how we would be received, but in fact we were received very graciously, and it seemed that no offence had been taken from my failure to visit the DO earlier.

John brought with him a report about the urine tests done on Helen, but unfortunately it was not clearly worded, so Glenys was unable to decide whether the infection had been cleared up or not. She felt that further tests were required, so off I cycled to the Adventist Hospital to see whether the tests could be done there. They could not. John had gone over to Abua for one night, and was planning to go to Joinkrama the following day for an overnight visit, so we decided to take advantage of his journey to accompany him and find out if the required tests could be done at the Baptist hospital there. We went with him to Mbiama in the VW, on the way dropping Big Helen for the last time, as near to her village as we could get on the surfaced road. From Mbiama we travelled upstream to Joinkrama in a launch from the hospital. There we were warmly received and fed by Dr. Norman and his family but found that this hospital was not equipped to do the tests either. The Norman children had some rabbits, and these were very popular with Helen, as she could walk under their hutches and tickle their toes. The launch was going back to Mbiama in the afternoon, so John gave us the VW keys and we were able to return home the same day. It rained hard during the return journey on the launch and we all got soaked, though this did not prevent Helen from going happily to sleep.

The following day we had to make a decision: should Glenys take Helen back to Enugu with John? We decided that since the opportunity for a ride there was not likely to recur soon, this was the safest thing to do. So we drove the VW into Ahoada to borrow Alicia's suitcase again, and discovered that Roy would be going to Enugu a week or so later in his car and would be able to bring Glenys and Helen back again. That really sealed our decision, and Glenys began packing while I drove to Mbiama to meet John off the launch from Joinkrama. Joy and Elaine were also travelling to Enugu to help teach on a course being held there, so the VW was comfortably full.

After they had all gone, I had plenty to do by way of tidying things up, but still felt rather flat and drained in the evening. It was a relief to know that Helen would be able to have the appropriate attention, but not so good to be unexpectedly left on my own. Several people from the village came by to enquire after the family, and the general conclusion was, "It remain yourself alone, sah." That evening as I was washing up, a couple of little girls aged about nine or ten came to the kitchen window to chat, and to give a running commentary on everything I did. However when they learnt that Glenys and Helen had gone to Enugu and that I was alone, one of them said very innocently and sympathetically, "Never mind, Big Helen will sleep with you." I was glad to be able to tell them that Big Helen was not there either, and would not be coming back. Our minds had been so set on Baby Helen's problems, that we had never considered the implications of my being alone in the house if Big Helen had still been with us. The two little girls instructed me to shut the windows carefully before I went to bed, and promised to come and talk to me again another day. Such kind concern was very cheering!

It was during this week when I was alone that an offer of help came from Seven, the quiet young man who lived in the house nearest to ours. We had seen him around often enough, but he lived on his own and kept himself to himself, so his offer was something of a surprise. But with Bob now partially occupied with being a houseboy and Reverend away for a month, it was good to have someone else to call on for language work. Despite having only the basic six years of formal education, Seven was to prove himself an adept and conscientious helper. Moreover, by now we had some knowledge of the dialect situation in Ekpeye. Everyone seemed to agree that there were four main dialects, of which Reverend spoke one and Bob another. Seven was a speaker of a third, so any difference between his speech and that of Reverend or Bob would be a matter of interest. In fact, the differences turned out to be minor, and there was no difficulty of communication between any of the four dialects.

Why Seven was so called never became clear. Bob told me that his real name was "Spera in Deo," Latin for "Hope in God," though this seemed difficult to believe. We never met anyone else with a Latin motto for a name, and it was very hard to imagine how such a phrase could have reached Orupata. On the other hand, if Bob was wrong, where did he get the Latin motto from? Seven himself claimed that his official name was Okparanta, so we took his word for it. Nobody ever called him anything but Seven, so it did not really matter, and was conveniently left as another of life's little mysteries.

One evening while I was alone, I had put out the pressure lamp and was just getting ready to go to bed when by the feeble light of the bat lamp I noticed something long and thin curled up on the bedroom floor near the end of the bed. It looked suspiciously like a snake. I stood and watched it carefully for some minutes but in the meagre light of the bat lamp I could not make out clearly either a head or a tail. It did not seem to be moving, but I had no desire to share the bedroom with a serpent, and wanted to be sure. Eventually I fetched the broom, and gingerly prodded the object with the broom handle. It still did not move, so I picked it up on the end of the handle, to realise with some relief that it was only an old inner tube from a bicycle wheel, presumably put through the bedroom window by some miscreant child. Since the window overlooked the path to Good's house, I could make an educated guess about who the miscreant might be. If this was his revenge for his imprisonment, then I had to admit that it was both ingenious and effective. But I never gave him the satisfaction of knowing that his trick had worked so well.

In the event my period of solitude was not as long as we had expected. After a few days, Peter, the oil company surveyor, turned up saying that he was going to Enugu for the weekend, and offering to take me with him. This was too good a chance to miss, so on the Friday afternoon I arrived unannounced at the SIL house in Enugu, to the surprise and delight of Glenys and especially Helen. On the way I learnt more about Peter's reasons for making the journey. He explained that he was looking for some survey markers, somewhere in the bush about twenty miles from Enugu, and buried four feet underground. This did not seem to me very precise directions, so we were not surprised to hear later that he never found them. What did surprise us was his disappointment.

The news that greeted me about Helen was good. Glenys had been able to see the doctor who had treated Helen earlier, and with a change of medication, she was already much improved. In fact the problem did not recur. This unplanned visit to Enugu also gave us the chance to finalise our arrangements for returning home in September, which we had not been able to do earlier. Rather than going straight back to England, we were planning to travel via Greece to visit some friends, so the journey was not as simple as it might have been. Moreover the time was approaching when we would have to make some proposals for establishing an official script for Ekpeye, and John was able to provide some helpful ideas on how to go about this, so the weekend was a very fruitful one. Roy collected us as planned after the weekend and we were soon back in Orupata, much easier in our minds about Helen's welfare.

Hardly were we back however, when I sat on my glasses and dislodged a lens from the frame. The nearest optician was in Port Harcourt fifty miles away, but Peter again came to our rescue. He was making a trip there the day after I damaged the glasses, so he took them with him and brought them back a couple of days later, repaired free of charge. He was planning to live with us for a while, and had already installed his generator, but didn't quite get round to coming himself. In fact a colleague of his called Michael stayed for a couple of nights before Peter finally showed up. His delay was not inconvenient as we had another short absence planned, this time to visit Amos Udonsak, our Nigerian fellow-student who had come to see us off at Euston Station the previous July. He was now at home again, working as the Principal of a Bible College in a town called Abak, and had invited us to visit him for a couple of days.

Amos came to Orupata to collect us in a rather rickety taxi, and our journey of about 130 miles to Abak was accomplished with nothing worse than a puncture, and frequent stops to refill the leaking radiator. We were happy to meet his wife Naomi and three of his four children aged 12, 10 and 7 (the oldest was away at secondary school), and were both impressed and amused to find the children lined up to bid us "Good morning" and "Good evening" at the appropriate times. We wanted to take photos of the family, but Naomi would not be photographed. She felt that because she was pregnant a photo would be unflattering. In due course we heard that she safely delivered a little boy.

We enjoyed an unexpected meal that Naomi provided for us of sausage, chips and beans. By now we knew enough to realise that none of these would have been easily available locally, so it was a real treat. Breakfasts on the two following mornings were large and fried, but being out of practice with such meals, Glenys was strangely unable to enjoy them or do them proper justice. Since fresh milk was no more available in Abak than in Ahoada, Amos thoughtfully provided tins of evaporated milk for us to use in tea or coffee. Glenys has always disliked evaporated milk, but it would have been ungracious to turn it down, so she just had to swallow it as best she could. Drinking was thus a duty rather than a pleasure, a distinct drawback in a hot climate.

On our one full day with him, Amos took us the 16 miles to Etinan where the mission he worked with had a hospital and secondary school. The secondary school contained a well equipped biology laboratory, complete with pickled snakes and so on. The hospital, with 150 beds, was large compared with the one at Ika, but had only one over-worked doctor. As we toured the hospital, Glenys saw her first case of kwashiorkor, a dietary deficiency that was not prevalent in the Ekpeye area. The hospital secretary cum almoner was a Miss Bunting, whose parents lived next door to us in Kentish Town when we were first married. We had never met her before, but on the basis of this tenuous connection, she invited us all to lunch. She was the proud possessor of an adult tricycle, which was very useful in getting around the large hospital compound, and which we enjoyed attempting to ride. Riding an adult tricycle, and particularly steering it, is more difficult than people who have never tried it expect, and we certainly had our fun, as well as providing free entertainment for any onlookers..

On the way home in the same taxi we stopped at Ikot Ekpene, where there was a shop selling locally made artefacts at very reasonable prices. We bought a few items including some carved calabashes (a type of gourd) that still decorate our house to this day, a happy memory of a very enjoyable reunion with our good friend Amos.

Chapter 13
Hotel Orupata

When we reached home again, we were mildly surprised to find Ian and Amelia ensconced there, and cooking themselves some soup. Since Bob knew very well who they were, he had not hesitated to let them into the house in our absence. They had brought Alison Ruth to have her vaccination at the Adventist Hospital, and spent a night with us before returning to Abua. The following day we were entertained by an eclipse of the sun, which we managed to observe by looking through two pairs of sun glasses. The local reaction to this event was a mixture of modern scientific interest and ancient anxieties.

It was around this time that the unpredictable Peter actually stayed a few nights with us, and one very happy outcome of this was that he became aware that Roy and Alicia needed a new night watchman, or "watch-night" as they were called locally. Enoch had recently given up his job in order to live at home and support his wife, so we were happy to recommend him as a conscientious and reliable man, and he got the job. Alicia was aware of the precarious situation with Enoch's twins, and this may well have been a factor in their decision. Anyway we were very pleased to have been able to give some practical help to both parties. Enoch was still in the job when we left Orupata.

Peter's departure was no less unpredictable than his presence. The day before he was due to leave, he had been paying off his men in Ahoada, and somehow in the process the sum of four pounds had been stolen so that there was not enough money to pay everyone. The identity of the thief was known, and his colleagues wanted to beat him up, but Peter would not let them. They then wanted to beat Peter up. This resulted in a near riot, but somehow Peter managed to get himself and the thief to the Police Station, where they spent half the night trying to sort the matter out. A court case was due to take place the next morning, and this required more formal attire than usual. But Peter discovered to his consternation that he had no long trousers with him at our house. He was several inches taller than me, and would have looked absurd in my trousers, so he had to rush off and borrow a pair from Roy. The thief got 18 months hard labour, which seemed to us a rather draconian punishment for the theft of four pounds, but at least Peter was able to leave the area in one piece.

Bob had recruited a twelve year old cousin of his from Ekpena village called Israel to help with looking after

Helen. He didn't speak much English, though this hardly mattered as Helen was quite at home with communication in Ekpeye. Israel worked with us for a couple of weeks and seemed to be coping reasonably well. Then Bob announced that Israel's family had decided he should leave us forthwith and go to Joinkrama to look after his sister's child there. This was very irritating, so in an act of undisguised economic imperialism we decreed that unless Israel worked with us till the end of the month, he would get no pay. Bob was our intermediary in this palaver, and like so many palavers, it ended in a compromise. Israel stayed with us till the end of the week, and we paid him not for the full month but just for the days he had actually worked. Since these were reduced by our absences in Enugu and Abak, which we would have overlooked if he had worked the full month, he did not get very much. We had the impression that he did not really want to go to Joinkrama, where he would get his board and food but no wages, so this whole situation was a bit hard on him, but his family had to realise that unilateral decisions may have multilateral consequences.

To our surprise our neighbour Seven volunteered to fill the unexpected vacancy, and as he was on good terms both with Helen and with Bob, we accepted his offer. He had already taken to spending half the day reclining in one of the two wooden armchairs that Peter that discarded on our verandah, so we thought that if Seven was going to be in our house anyway, he might as well be working. He gradually began to help us as well with our language studies, proving himself to be a capable story-teller, and became a quiet but valuable helper in several ways.

One day Helen fell over in the house and banged her head against a door. For a few days she sported a black eye, but there was no lasting damage. Her speech continued to develop apace, and one aspect of this was a phase in which she repeated everything we said to her. This was normally no problem, though it was hard for us to maintain serious expressions if we were trying to tell her off for some misdemeanour or other, and all our rebukes came straight back to us. One day she overheard me saying to our hen, "If you don't produce some eggs soon, we'll chop you" (the local expression for "eat"). A couple of days later, she was seen with a packet of Robin starch in her hand, with a brightly coloured robin on it, at which she wagged her finger and said "I'll chop you." She also fancied herself as a music critic. One day I was humming a tune while we ate our tea, and Helen commented to Glenys, "Daddy sing *mano-o*" ("no good" in Ekpeye). Indeed, even my best friends would not give me a high rating as a singer. Glenys had made a little white dress for Helen, and added a pocket with an outline of an elephant embroidered on it. Helen was very proud of her new pocket, and went around for some time with her hand in the pocket. Eventually she filled it with sand, and the white dress was never quite so white again.

The time had come to try to set up an Ekpeye orthography committee which could examine the various possible ways of writing the language, and make recommendations about which way was most acceptable. To this end Reverend took me one day to meet a man in Ahoada with the title of Educational Assistant, a Mr. Nebu. He was interested and helpful, and agreed to chair the committee, so I began drafting invitations to people whom Mr. Nebu proposed as suitable members of the committee, mainly local primary school headmasters. There was a good response, and on the agreed day early in June we all gathered at the Anglican school in Ahoada. The meeting was scheduled for two o'clock in the afternoon, but it was about quarter to three before we got going. I was invited to set out the specific difficulties of deciding on an appropriate writing system for Ekpeye. The recommendations I had to make for writing consonants were accepted after some discussion. There was nothing controversial in them anyway. The real problem lay in the vowels.

Ekpeye had nine distinct vowel sounds and of course roman script offers only five vowel letters, so the tough decision is how to write the other four vowels. In Ekpeye, the nine vowels fall into two sets of four, plus the vowel "a." In most nouns all the vowels come from either one set or the other, with "a" going happily with both sets. This kind of patterning is quite common in West Africa, and is known as vowel harmony. My suggestion was that e, i, o and u should be used for one vowel set, and the same letters with an underline (e̲, i̲, o̲ and u̲) should be used for the other set. The advantage of this was that it is fairly easy to produce underlines on a typewriter, so the system is quite practical. The drawback was that the major language of Eastern Nigeria, Igbo, to which Ekpeye was related, used a system of underdots rather than underlines to make up the three extra vowel letters it needed (i̟, o̟ and u̟) to write its eight vowels. Inevitably there was a desire by some Ekpeye people to make their language look like the most prestigious language of the region. Underdots are more difficult to produce on a typewriter, and are less visible anyway, so in Igbo the result was that most people did not bother to put them in at all. For this reason three important vowel contrasts were usually lost in writing. Another possibility for Ekpeye was to use a combination of vowel plus h to make up the four extra characters (eh, ih, oh and uh) but this would produce a page with h occurring so many times that it was visually very unattractive. The vowel question was left unanswered at the first committee meeting, and people went away to think about the problem.

Some days later an Igbo man came to visit me in the village, to express his interest in developing a writing system for Ekpeye. He brought with him a little book he had written entitled "Ekpeye and English in a Modern Authography"(!). He had chosen to write one set of vowels with an underline, just as I had proposed to the orthography committee, and he gave numerous words to illustrate his suggested spelling system. The only drawback was that the printer had not put in a single underline anywhere in the book, a salutary warning to me that underlines were no more likely to be successful than underdots! (In writing this book for readers who do not know Ekpeye, I have put all Ekpeye words in italics. However, I must confess that I have taken the line of least resistance, and simply abandoned the distinction between the two sets of vowels, much as it goes against my linguistic conscience to do so!)

A short while later a second meeting of the orthography committee was held, but those attending included a number who had not been present the first time, so I had to explain some of the basic issues all over again. Participation was eager and voluble, and in the end it was more or less agreed to give a trial to the system of writing the vowels that I had proposed. This was to be evaluated at a third meeting a couple of months later.

On a more personal level, one day Bob took me aside, and said in a manner that contrived to be both sheepish and conspiratorial, "Sah, I am hearin' in de village dat Madam is under conception." I was rather taken aback by this news. Presumably some of the women in the village had seen what size Helen was, and on the basis of their own experience with children, had decided that it was high time for *Ina* Helen to start producing her next offspring. Bob had evidently been commissioned to find out if their calculations were correct. I gave him a non-committal reply, but within a couple of weeks we realised that the village women were right, and Glenys was indeed expecting again. In retrospect, that was the reason for her nausea at the cooked breakfasts that Amos' wife had gone to such trouble to provide us with, but at the time we had not realised it. Before long Glenys had to make a trip to the market in Ahoada to buy a wrap-around cloth that would readily accommodate varying degrees of gradual expansion. Both Alicia and Amelia passed on the kind of "bell tent" maternity smocks that were more common then than they are now, and very comfortable they proved in a hot and sticky climate. One day a woman we did not know came to our house, looked around for a few minutes and then left again. Bob told us she was checking up on Glenys to make sure she really was pregnant. If she had not been, perhaps my reputation would have been under threat.

A couple of weeks later we had guests for a less happy reason. Amelia had developed serum hepatitis, probably contracted from an unsterile needle when she was given an injection at the time Alison was born in Nsukka. So Gary, the Peace Corps volunteer, brought the whole family over to us. Ian and Timothy stayed with us, while Amelia and Alison were transferred to the Adventist Hospital. Helen and Timothy were more than happy to have each other's company, and played well together most of the time. Ian would cycle out to the hospital each day, and spend the nights with us.

One day Helen and Timothy were playing in a pile of sand that lay in our front yard, and discovered some eggs in it. We had a few anxious moments wondering whether they were gecko's eggs or possibly snake's eggs, so we took one and tried to open it. It was surprisingly rubbery and difficult to open, but when we got it open, we were relieved to see it was only a gecko inside. On another occasion Helen brought a snail to us, fascinated to see the head move when poked with a stick.

Timothy's behaviour was rather more adventurous than Helen's, and we found him one day brandishing an open pen-knife of Ian's. Ian had enough on his mind, so I quietly confiscated the knife, and later hid it among Ian's belongings, but out of Timothy's sight. Timothy was also more mobile than Helen at the meal table, probably because she was partially restrained by a child seat and he was not. One tea time as he leaned across the table I had to bark at him, "Timothy, take your fingers out of the Golden Syrup and sit down!" To everyone's surprise, he did, and thereafter seemed to live in awe of Helen's sergeant-majorish Daddy.

In our preparations for returning to England, we had been thinking about acquiring a car, and Roy informed us that if we ordered it from outside the United Kingdom, we would qualify for a discount. This seemed an attractive idea, so when Roy next made a trip to Port Harcourt, he took us with him to visit the Ford dealership, where the manager was a friend of his, a Swiss fellow called Karl. As a result of this we committed ourselves to buy a Cortina Estate car, which would be delivered to us on arrival in England, or so we were told.

June saw the return to Ahoada of the Southern Baptist missionary who was normally resident there, but had been away on leave since before we arrived. This was Miss Jo Scaggs, who had already served over twenty five years in the Niger Delta area, and was much loved by the Ekpeye people. The exact date of her return was a matter of some uncertainty. One Sunday morning Okpara announced that she would be visiting Orupata "by two o'clock sharp or three o'clock latest." We felt that such imprecision need not deter us from taking our siesta, and we were proved right, as it turned out that she had had some problem renewing her visa, and was actually still in the USA.

But Jo really did return some days later, and we were very glad to meet her at last, as we had heard a lot about her. She was very interested in the language work in Abua, Ekpeye and Engenni and did all she could to help and encourage the language workers. This was well illustrated one Sunday soon after her return. She attended the morning service in the Baptist church in Orupata, at which she was presented with a hen as a token of welcome. She then took Ian back to Ahoada in her Land Rover, and lent it to him to drive out to the hospital to collect Amelia, who was now a less virulent shade of yellow, and had been declared fit enough to return to Abua. Ian brought Amelia and Alison to us for lunch, then I accompanied them to Abua in order to drive the Land Rover back to Jo. Finally she dropped me in Orupata on her way to another village for an evening service, more than happy to have been able to help with the transportation.

Our house felt quite empty without Ian and Timothy. Without any planning on our part or theirs, their stay had fitted neatly between short but unpredictable visits from Peter, from Godwin and from Maurice. If everyone had turned up at the same time, we would not have had enough beds for them all.

Mother-of-Good produced a new baby at this time and of course we visited her to give our congratulations, and also for Glenys to make a surreptitious check on the baby's welfare. Happily it did not have the same deformity as its elder brother. As new life was given to a neighbour's family, so older life was taken away from our own. Within the space of a few weeks we received news of the deaths in England of an aunt of mine and an uncle of Glenys'. Inevitably the funerals were over before we even learnt of the deaths, and such events made us realise how far from home we were, and how remote from sharing family sorrows.

Chapter 14
A Brush with the Law

When we returned from visiting Amos, it was to find that while we had been away *Ina* Anti, Alice, had finally done what she had been planning for a long time, and had "gone to Spanish" to join her husband. Her house was occupied by a relative of hers, a single fellow by the name of Eze. As far as we were concerned he kept himself to himself, but we did get the impression that his presence was not entirely welcome to other people in the vicinity. There were no specific complaints, but we gathered that he was what was euphemistically known as a rogue.

One day about five weeks later, Bob came to us and told us he thought that Eze was drying Indian hemp behind his house. Even as long ago as 1966, well before drug abuse became the curse it is today, we were aware that this was the plant from which marijuana was made, and that if Bob was right, this was an activity illegal in Nigeria. When Eze was absent, Bob took a small sample of the dubious plant and brought it to me. Neither Glenys nor I had ever seen the plant before, and we could not identify it with any confidence, but the possibility that we might be living cheek by jowl with a drug producer raised the question of what if anything we should do about it. At least we now began to understand something of the reservations that other people had about the new neighbour. Ian was still with us when the problem came to our attention, so we were able to discuss it with him, and we all felt that this was not just something to which we should turn a blind eye. Drug use was a growing problem in Nigeria and newspapers carried numerous reports of people being caught with marijuana.

So next day I furtively wrapped up the sample of the suspicious plant and, feeling rather like a criminal myself, cycled off to seek the advice of the District Officer. Unknown to us however, the day I had chosen turned out to be a public holiday, and neither the DO nor his assistant were anywhere to be found. But my journey was not entirely wasted, as I had the chance to visit Jo Scaggs and ask her advice. She too felt that the matter was serious enough that it should not be ignored. So next day I cycled in again to try to find the DO. I was just in time as he was about to go on leave. He quickly handed me over to the local police inspector, whose office was near his own, and the inspector handed me over to the CID sergeant. The sergeant was quickly able to identify the plant as Indian hemp, and decided to take prompt action. I was told to return home, while two plain clothes constables were given directions to our home, and were detailed to follow me at a suitable interval.

What followed was like something from a spoof police movie. I had not been home long when the two burly constables rode up to the house, inspected the layout of the nearby houses, and announced that they would use our house as a base from which to watch for the rogue. They seemed quite content to leave their shiny new bikes in our front yard in full view of everyone. We gently pointed out that as their bikes were much better than the average village bike, the rogue might spot them and disappear before giving any reason to be arrested. The constables accepted the logic of this and agreed that it would be a good idea to bring their bikes inside our house out of sight. Perhaps they had just not liked to ask permission to do this. Once it was done, and they had been given a drink of water, we unlocked the side gate of the back garden. This meant that they could lurk among the sugar canes and keep a close eye on the house next door while remaining out of sight behind the wall that surrounded the garden. And they could make a quick pounce through the back gate at need. A pile of hemp leaves drying in the sun was clearly visible behind Alice's house, so the prospect of an arrest seemed good.

This whole procedure was of course of great interest and excitement to Bob. We felt that since the policemen had had to ride through Orupata market place to reach our house, their arrival was unlikely to have passed unnoticed, and the whole village would know about it very quickly. After a while Bob went up to the home of his relatives to eat with them. On the way Eze met him and actually asked him if there were any policemen in the village, so he evidently had his suspicions. Bob said he did not know since he had left our house. Nevertheless about an hour later Eze came back stealthily to the house and went round the back to inspect the leaves. The two constables leapt out of our back gate, sprinted the few yards to the next garden and had the rogue under arrest in no time, caught red-handed – or perhaps in this case green-handed. There were a number of witnesses to the arrest including ourselves and Ian, and we even managed to take some photos. As far as we could judge, most people were pleased to see Eze being taken away. In particular *Ina* Chika was dancing with joy. Whether Eze had pestered her when her husband was away we did not know, but we could not help wondering. She was quite an attractive young woman.

The constables had to frog-march Eze the two miles back to Ahoada, but they were fit young men, and seemed more elated at the success of their investigation than worried about the long walk in the heat. Bob was of course thrilled with the turn of events, and began to fantasise about the outcome. After the inevitable conviction the two constables, he assured us, would be promoted, and in gratitude would come back and reward me with gifts of money. This was not at all my vision for the future, and I said it would be more use if they helped Bob to get a job in the police. Neither outcome seemed at all likely, though some years later we heard through Ian that Bob had in fact joined the police.

The two policemen's bikes remained in our house until the evening, when they came back for them. They then told us that when Eze was charged at the police station, he had pleaded not guilty and denied that the hemp was his at all. Even worse, in his statement he claimed that it belonged to Bob, perhaps feeling that Bob had deceived him about the presence of the police in the village. Naturally Bob was rather worried by this, but the policemen reassured him, and took his own statement denying that he had anything to do with the hemp. We did not advertise the fact that it was Bob who had drawn my attention to the hemp in the first place, in case anyone in Orupata felt inclined to take revenge on him. Rather strangely, nobody appeared to realise that I was the person who had tipped off the police, and we were content to let the situation stay that way.

Inevitably in a village community, Eze had a number of relatives, but despite this, the reactions that came to us about his arrest were favourable ones. The most insightful comment came from Enoch, who said, "He is my relative, but he is a bad man." So many people would have put it the other way round, and given relationship priority over behaviour. It transpired that although Eze was still quite young, he had already served one jail sentence for a previous conviction, though we were not sure what the offence was in that case. We learnt on the grapevine that there were at least two other people in Orupata who were involved in growing hemp, but we had no idea who they were, and since it was not going on under our noses, we did not feel obliged to make enquiries. It was up to the police to investigate if they wanted to make further arrests.

The consequences of this arrest rumbled on beyond the duration of our stay in Orupata. A week or so after the excitement, Bob told us that another rogue in the village had "threatened his life" in connection with the case. It was a bit scary for him, but Bob did not give in to intimidation, and never suggested that it was time for him to leave us and return to his own village. Not long after receiving this threat, Bob informed us that the second rogue had "stolen a trousah and run to Onitsha." We knew what Bob meant of course, but still savoured the vision of a villain with one bare leg jogging guiltily along the 150-mile road to Onitsha.

A couple of weeks after the arrest, one of the policemen came back to receive copies of the photos we had taken, and after a couple more weeks a rumour reached us that Eze had been let out on bail. This was probably not true, as he never returned to the house next to ours, and was in custody when the case came up for its first hearing in

August. Bob and I had gone in to the Ahoada court house in the morning for an eight o'clock start, but when the case came up about half past nine, the result was an anti-climax: it was postponed till September. We suspected that the real reason for this was that the accused had not paid his solicitor's fees, but there was nothing we could do about that. The magistrate in Ahoada turned out to be a man we could not fail to notice whenever we saw him about the town, because he had the distinction very unusual in Africa of being an albino.

A few days before the next hearing was due, Bob came to tell us that he thought someone in Orupata was trying to put a spell on him, presumably in connection with the hemp case. His reason for thinking this was that he had found a large stone half buried in our front yard, and an elderly relative of his had declared it to be "juju." Why Bob assumed it was directed against himself rather than against us was not clear. Anyway he did not seem unduly worried by it and we tried to reassure him that if he was a Christian, no juju spell could harm him even if it succeeded in harming those who believed in it and feared it. At any rate Bob was not smitten down by any mysterious disease, and neither were we, so if anyone had intended evil against any of us, they were disappointed.

Eventually the day arrived for the second hearing of the case, which was number eleven on the list of cases to be tried that day. Bob and I waited around outside the court house all the morning, but to our chagrin only ten cases had been heard by the time the court rose, so the case was left in abeyance again. I managed to have a word with Eze's solicitor, and was happy to learn that he had never heard of Bob, so evidently the specious allegation that the hemp had belonged to Bob had been dropped by the accused. The solicitor also made it clear that he did not consider his client had any chance of being acquitted, and that was something we were happy to know. The case now had no possibility of being heard before we returned to England, and from one point of view this was a relief to us. If, as seemed likely, Eze received another jail sentence and any of his relatives or fellow rogues felt like taking it out on Bob, at least Bob would no longer be in Orupata after our departure, but back in the safety of his own village, Ekpena.

Some months later we heard that the case had been settled and that Eze had received ten years in prison. We had no means of checking whether this was accurate, and we were inclined to doubt it since stories were easily exaggerated in the telling. If it were true, it seemed an extremely heavy punishment, even for someone who was not a first offender. But the sentence would not have been served in full anyway, because during the Biafran war that began less than a year later, prisoners were freed in order to be conscripted into the army.

Had we done the right thing in bringing this matter to the attention of the police, or were we interfering in local matters in a way that went beyond our responsibilities as foreigners? Roy was of the opinion that we should just have burnt the hemp and told Eze not to grow it again. If that had worked, it might have been a simpler and quicker solution. If it had not worked, it could have left us in a very vulnerable position, something that with a small child to care for would have been highly undesirable. The general reaction of other people in Orupata made us feel that we had adopted the course of action that entailed the fewest problems, and treated Nigerian law seriously. But we were glad not to have to face any other similar decisions.

Chapter 15
Loose Ends

The court case was by no means the only aspect of our lives that was dangling in a tantalising way. As the weeks passed, we became ever more aware that our time in Orupata was limited. It began to seem increasingly unlikely that we would be able to do as much study as we wanted, or at least to complete as much analysis of the language as we had hoped. Some days the situation seemed hopeless, and it was easy to fall into bouts of pessimism, as practically any post-graduate student discovers. At such times, an uneventful suburban existence in England seemed like Shangri-la. However this kind of fantasizing was no way to make the most of our remaining time, and we generally managed not to become too desperate.

On the language side, we began to give priority to tape recording stories from various people. Most of them were folk tales, though there were also some accounts of personal experiences. It was of course at this period that, with the intrinsic cussedness that always seems to be built into gadgets of any kind, the microphone of our tape recorder became very temperamental. This was most frustrating when people came from other villages to tell stories for us to record, as we could not expect them to come back on some other day when the microphone chose to co-operate. It was sent to Enugu for attention, but returned without much improvement. I was able to borrow microphones from other people at various times, and gradually the stockpile of recorded stories increased to satisfactory proportions. In a few cases the quality of the recording was so poor that it could not be used, but most of the texts could be heard well enough to be transcribed.

This was where Bob made himself indispensable. As a mother tongue speaker of Ekpeye, he had a much quicker and more accurate appreciation than Glenys or I could ever have of what the speakers on the tapes were saying, especially if the story was one he had told himself, or had heard someone else telling. Because of this he spent a lot of time during our last few weeks together transcribing the recorded stories onto paper. He had worked with us for long enough that he had understood the principles of the way we wrote Ekpeye words for our own purposes, so he was able to spell his own language well, perhaps better than any other speaker at that time.

Reverend had made a start on translating the Gospel of Mark into Ekpeye, and we were able to spend some time with him checking a few chapters of his work against the original Greek. Since he had not studied Greek himself, he had to work from an English translation. Although his English was pretty good, we did discover one rather entertaining misunderstanding. In Jesus' parable of the sower, the seed lands on four different kinds of soil, with four different results. The last of the four pictures is of seed falling among thorns, which "grew up and choked it" (Mark 4.7). Reverend thought that the English verb "to choke" was the same as the pidgin word "to chuke," which means to lacerate, penetrate or puncture.

We had learnt this word one day when Okpara had come limping along to get some medical help from Glenys. He had fallen off his bicycle, and one pedal had given him a nasty cut on the sole of his foot. Okpara described the mishap with the statement "Dis *igwe* done chuke me for foot." Glenys applied some antiseptic ointment and a bandage and he soon recovered. We stored away the word "chuke" for future reference, and now it came in useful. Reverend was not familiar with the English word "choke" which in the context of plants growing, is used in a metaphorical sense anyway. The literal meaning of "chuke" is not entirely out of place in the context of thorns, and he had pictured the thorns actually penetrating the stems of the wheat that was growing from the seeds sown by the farmer. So the general sense of his translation was not misleading, though in detail he had not grasped the exact force of the original parable. This was a memorable lesson to us of the importance of having a correct understanding of any text that is to be translated from one language to another. How well did we understand the Ekpeye stories that we were so busy recording? Fortunately we did not have to rely on our own unaided knowledge, as Bob and Seven were around to help correct our misunderstandings, just as we tried to help Reverend.

In July my birthday came round again, and was celebrated in a very different way from the previous one in Sierra Leone. The celebration was now marked not by luxurious shipboard food, but by tinned chicken, packet mashed potatoes and tinned peas, with tinned pears and cream to follow. We had few tinned goods, so opening a tin was in itself the mark of a red letter day. For tea Glenys made a sponge, iced it and decorated it with a rather inaccurate twenty-one candles. The evening was marked by another ant attack, but the would-be boarders were spotted in time to be repelled with insecticide spray. A few days later Jo called in and presented us with half an apple pie. The apples had probably come from Port Harcourt, but we were not troubled by such mundane questions in the face of an unexpected treat.

We were by now thinking about some souvenirs to take home, and Samuel recommended a carver in Ahoada whom we commissioned to produce what for some reason was called a Zorro head. This was a head with vertically elongated hair carved in hard wood, said to be ebony, but probably something cheaper. There was a hole drilled through the centre so that the head could be threaded with flex and turned into a lamp. The head is still with us, but the whole thing was top heavy and the base was not completely flat, so it never became a lamp.

There were fewer novelties from the animal world by this stage. Bob did see a small snake in our back garden one day, but it escaped before he could get something to kill it with, and it was not seen again. The water in the swamp in the rainy season had plenty of tadpoles in it, and we had a few in a glass jar for Helen to watch as they developed. One day I saw a large one in the act of eating a smaller one, but I did not draw her attention to this. Helen had her own contacts with the world of small creatures, and one day passed a large roundworm. Glenys had some medicine to give her, but no more worms appeared, so the infestation was not serious.

The frequent rains brought the temperature down a little at nights, so we put Helen into a pair of cotton pyjamas instead of the nightie she had always worn before. She was delighted with her outlandish new garb, and was particularly fascinated by the buttons on the jacket. No sooner was the jacket put on and the buttons done up than the buttons had to be undone so that the jacket could come off again. And of course as soon as it was off, it had to be put back on again so that the buttons could be done up. Her enthusiasm for this kind of game rapidly exceeded ours.

Helen's speech continued to develop in a mixture of Ekpeye, pidgin and English. I developed a boil in one ear that was quite painful until Glenys lanced it. Helen was aware of Daddy's discomfort, and would ask solicitously in pidgin "Get pain for ear?" This would be followed by "*Nyeke-o*," an expression of sympathy in Ekpeye. When she herself had a new pair of sandals, they rubbed her feet a bit at first. Feeling sorry for herself, she took them off and said "Poor Baby! Smack shoe-shoes." She also picked up the Igbo word for God, *Chineke*, which was not infrequently used as an exclamation in Ekpeye. However she clearly did not understand it, as we heard her saying to herself one evening when she was in her cot, "I want Chineke." At this period, Helen began to take an interest in telling the time, but it was always either "twenty past" or "half past" as these were the only times she knew. One morning, she issued the command "Daddy, get up. Clock says half past twenty." One has to wonder what is going on in the minds of children when they use expressions that they clearly do not understand.

In preparation for our impending return to *ul'ibheke* ("village of white man") as people called England, we made a practice of showing Helen photos of various members of the family at regular intervals, so that when she met them, they would not seem like strangers. She soon learnt to identify them, especially the grandparents, and then proceeded to identify with them anybody she saw in photos in odd copies of the Reader's Digest that we had. In some cases the relatives might have been flattered, and in others not.

The wet season was the wrestling season in Ekpeye, and wrestling among young men was a highly regarded sport with its own rules. The village had two main teams of wrestlers, and it was an interesting reflection of what was counted as prestigious in the village that the two teams called themselves "The Russians" on one side, and "Shell" (the oil company) on the other. The two teams consisted of age-sets, that is groups of young men all born within a year or two of each other. These age-sets were quite important social units. Competitions took place at intervals in the *unama* or "playground" as people called it in English, a public square in the main part of the village, not far from the tree where the weaver birds lived. We went along from time to time to watch, especially if Seven was participating. He was one of the Russians, and there was great rejoicing one day when his group managed to defeat Shell, especially as the Shell team came from a senior age-set. Helen was very fond of Seven by this time, and became quite anxious if she saw him competing, especially if he got thrown. On one occasion she stood at the edge of the competition area growling at his opponent, and had to be restrained from rushing out to "rescue" him.

Seven always insisted that he was thirteen years old, though to us it was obvious that he was older than that.

In England teenagers usually like to be thought older than they really are, and we could not understand Seven's reluctance to admit his true age. One day I sat down with him and asked, "Seven how old were you when you started school?"

"Six years old, sah," came the answer.

"And how many years did you go to school for?" I continued.

"Six years, sah."

"And how many years ago did you leave school?"

"Three years ago, sah."

"What is six plus six plus three?"

"Fifteen, sah."

"Then how old must you be?"

"I am thirteen years old, sah."

It was Reverend who eventually explained Seven's determination to be thirteen for ever and ever. At sixteen men became liable to pay the annual poll tax of one pound per head, and Seven wanted to postpone the evil day as long as possible. Mere arithmetic was powerless in the face of economic reality.

The occurrence of my birthday had made Bob consider his own birthday. His family had no record of exactly when he was born, so he was free to choose a date to his own satisfaction. He chose the 7th of September, and his rationale, like Seven's, was economic. We had arrived on the 8th of September in 1965, and he had told us then that he was "about 15." Therefore his sixteenth birthday could not be postponed later than the 7th of September 1966, when he bought himself a little bean-cake and stuck some candles in it. My brother in England was much the same age as Bob, so we arranged for him to send Bob a birthday card. It arrived safely, and the thrill of receiving the first birthday card he had ever had helped to sweeten the bitter pill of becoming a tax-payer. But with any luck Bob would still be able to "run for bush" when the tax collectors arrived.

Although our main goal was to study Ekpeye, it seemed useful to take some sample data from other related languages in the area. Neither Engenni to the west nor Abuan to the south-east were related to Ekpeye, but there were two other adjacent languages that were, namely Ikwere to the east and Ogba to the north. There was no need for me to travel to these areas, as native speakers of both languages were available in Ahoada. I was able to make contact with them, and in both cases found men willing and able to help me. The procedure was to elicit one hundred words from each language, following a list constructed by an American linguist called Morris Swadesh. At that time this list was widely used in gathering comparative data from related languages. One day a Mr. Azuma came to our house and provided the data for Ogba, and a couple of weeks later a Mr. Henshaw came and did the same for Ikwere. Both were good informants, clear speakers who had an intuitive grasp of the difficulties I faced in writing words in languages I had not studied. They were willing to repeat words when I hesitated over writing them, and were able to whistle the tones when I was uncertain about them.

I did not have much time to examine this data while we were still in Nigeria, but after we returned home, it became the basis for a seminar paper at SOAS. Later still, in 1971, a couple of years after my thesis was finished, it became the subject of the first academic paper I ever had published. Would I ever have bothered to write it up without the unexpected stimulus that Prof. Pike had provided at Nsukka? I don't know, but I still look back on this piece of work with nostalgia, and with gratitude for the encouragement of established scholars. As I have grown older, I have tried not to forget the importance of encouraging younger scholars as opportunity offers.

A number of medical cases came to Glenys' attention during our last few months in Orupata. One was a baby with pneumonia. All Glenys could do was tell the mother to take the child to the Adventist hospital, which rather to our surprise she did. The baby soon improved, and some weeks later the father came to Glenys with a nasty cut on his hand. Again she could only tell him to go to the hospital, and no doubt encouraged by the recovery of the baby, he also went. He was given both injections and stitches and in due course he too recovered.

Less satisfactory was the situation of a little girl of about three in a family that was one of our less immediate neighbours. She was the little sister of the boy called Young, and was known to us only as *Ol'ungwo* Young, junior sister of Young. She had a deep gash under her chin, probably caused by playing with a machete. Again Glenys had to tell the parents to take her to the hospital to have the wound stitched, but in this instance they did not go. Instead they had treatment from a local lady who was a traditional healer. By talking with this lady, Glenys discovered that the treatment was a poultice of boiled leaves that was changed at regular intervals. Since the leaves were boiled, Glenys was happy that they would be sterile, and other people assured her that wounds treated in this way did not become infected. Glenys kept an eye on *Ol'ungwo* Young, and indeed the wound did not fester, nor did the little girl appear to be in pain. She must have ended up with a scar under her chin that would have been sizeable, though not disfiguring. It was surprising that there were not more such small children with bad cuts, as they were often to be seen carrying the sharp machetes that were essential tools in every household. More than once we winced to see Chika, who could hardly have been more than three, running around with a machete, but as far as we knew he never came to any harm. We took good care that Helen did not play with such lethal weapons.

One day when I had gone to Ahoada, Glenys had an adventure of her own. As part of a local festival, a group of three or four men went around the village wearing masks with grass and leaves attached. They shook their heads to wave the grass, and any women who saw them were supposed to run away in terror, real or feigned. When the men approached our house, the neighbouring women ran away, but Glenys did not realise that this was expected of her too, so she stood her ground and watched the men with some curiosity. They were nonplussed by this unconventional behaviour, and were not sure how to handle it. As custom required, Glenys offered them a drink of cold water, which they accepted before leaving to find other women who were more easily scared.

The sight of the men waving their grass "fringes" probably shed some light on a habit Helen had picked up. She had straight fair hair that was cut in a fringe, and otherwise hung down below the level of her ears. She had recently discovered that if she ran towards other children shaking her head so that her hair flopped about, the other children would run away. We had noticed this, but had not attributed any significance to it, but perhaps the other children were aware of the ritually scary nature of the grassy masks, and saw in Helen's hair a likeness to them. Occasionally people would ask us how we made Helen's hair straight, and when we told them it just grew that way naturally, they seemed to think we were keeping some secret from them. Once or twice we said that when the house was closed up for the night, we would put Helen on the floor, one of us standing on her hair and the other pulling her legs. This explanation was regarded as no less likely than the idea that hair could be naturally straight.

When he was not working with us Seven was at this time occupied in refurbishing his small house, which involved the reconstruction of a couple of walls. The frame was sound but the walls needed replastering, a task in which some of his relatives helped. For a few days the house was uninhabitable, so Seven asked if he could move his bed into our house and share Bob's room. We had no objection, and in principle neither had Bob, but the logistical details produced a long and (to us) rather entertaining palaver between Bob and Seven. Bob's room was not large, and there was not a lot of space to manoeuvre in with regard to the position of the beds. Seven was adamant that he did not want to sleep with his feet towards the door. We were baffled by this, but he explained that it was because Ekpeye people regarded that as a suitable position only for a corpse. Bob on the other hand did not want his head near Seven's feet, though as far as we could judge this was more a question of dignity than of psychology. Eventually they managed to juggle the beds into positions that satisfied them both. Seven was not with us for long, so the matter was soon forgotten.

The political situation in Nigeria was deteriorating faster than we realised. There were anti-Igbo riots in the north around the end of May, and at the end of July, there were both further riots and a second military coup in which General Ironsi was killed. In our remote location and with no radio, we did not get prompt or accurate information, and until our copies of the Guardian Weekly arrived, we heard only rumours. In one such rumour, someone we had no reason to distrust assured us that he had personally seen General Ironsi alive in Umuahia some days later than what we eventually learnt to be the date of his death.

Inevitably in times of disruption, postal services were delayed, so we were always behind with the news. We began to wonder whether our plans for leaving Nigeria would be disrupted, but had no real option but to proceed with them anyway. However the sense of uncertainty was unsettling, and would have been more so if we had not been so busy. On one of his quick visits Peter told us that Shell employees were instructed not to send overseas mail in times of political crisis, as the Post Office would just take it out and burn it. We took this with a pinch of salt, but the next weekly letter we sent home never arrived, the only letter that went missing during our entire time in West Africa. The postal service in our experience was thus more reliable than we had expected, though even in normal times, it had had its quirks. One day I was in the Post Office in Ahoada and the man in front of me asked for half a dozen three-penny stamps, this being the standard price for an inland letter. Occasionally there were no three-penny stamps, and one had to make up the price with penny and tupenny ones. This time the postmaster beamed at the customer and announced with the air of one doing a favour to the world at large, "Today we have four-penny stamps" - and apparently nothing smaller. The customer was not pleased, though there was nothing he could but pay up or wait for a new supply of three-penny ones. Fortunately for me, I did not need three-penny stamps that day.

The political instability gave rise to some wild speculations on the part of certain expatriates, and even wilder plans for emergency evacuation. Roy declared that he knew exactly what he would do, though his straight face made it hard to know whether he was serious or not. His declared plan was drive down to Mbiama, hijack the pontoon bridge across the Orashi, release it from the chains that pulled it across the river, and float it downstream to the sea. I am neither an engineer nor a sailor, but this seemed to me a rather precarious undertaking. The pontoon had neither a power source nor steering gear, so how one would persuade it to go round the many bends in the river, or to stop when it reached the sea (if it ever did), were unexplained. *Chacun à son goût!* Fortunately the situation did not deteriorate suddenly, so in the event there was ample opportunity for those who wanted to leave the country to do so in an orderly way.

The orthography committee had a third meeting in August, and to my relief decided to try out a system of writing the vowels without using either underdots or underlines. What they chose was to write one set of vowels with the normal letters and the other set with the vowel plus an r. This was similar in principle to the proposal to write the second set with a following h, but seemed more acceptable to the Ekpeye speakers. Since there was no contrast between r and l, the symbol r was not needed as a consonant, and no confusion was likely to arise. The drawback was that if the system was used consistently every page would have a large number of occurrences of r. This decision was taken not long before our departure, so it was not practical for us to have any part in testing it. In the event, we never heard whether it was tested or not, and once the Biafran war started the following year, people had other things on their minds than testing orthographies.

Chapter 16
Leaving Nigeria

One of the organisational aspects of preparing to leave the village was making sure we had enough of the food items that were not obtainable locally, without having too much of anything. One item that Glenys discovered we had rather a lot of was curry powder, so we gradually increased both the frequency and the strength of our curry intake over the last few weeks. We had not expected that curry would be a favourite with a two-year-old, but Helen's capacity for it amazed us. While we were enjoying a really hot dish that brought us out in a sweat, Helen would sit there mopping up the same meal with every sign of enjoyment and no sign of any side effects at all.

Some of the affairs we had become involved with rumbled on without reaching any clear conclusion. The court case about the hemp was not settled. The orthography chosen for testing was not tested. Reverend had not completed the translation of the Gospel of Mark, so we could not finish checking it with him. There was nothing more we could do about these matters as the next steps in all cases were out of our hands. Our main task was to ensure that we had collected enough language data for me to work on once we had returned to England. To this end we kept on recording stories and accounts of personal experiences as much as we could, and Bob kept on transcribing them in every spare minute.

Time became ever more precious, and one of the steps I took to save some was to stop shaving. In retrospect it seems a futile, even a desperate, measure, but it did add as much as twenty minutes to the working day. The down side was that it did nothing to endear me to my wife, but her strictures I managed to endure. Only Peter, who had a beard himself, considered that I had taken a step in the right direction. Most people maintained a tactful silence on the subject which was more eloquent than words. Helen was more tolerant, and quite enjoyed having her tummy tickled by an incipient beard. This particular form of masochism was known as "a pumble," and for some reason required the removal of my glasses in order to reach the required combination of ecstasy and horror.

The added level of activity during the day was not accompanied by better sleep at nights. It was the wet season, and when Helen was not waking us up, we could rely on the sandflies to do so, usually around four o'clock in the morning. There was another big funeral in the village, and for several days we were woken early by a procession accompanied by drums, and Helen calling out

"I want to see people sing." It was not the most restful period of our lives.

One of the tasks we had to carry out was to dispose of the various goods and chattels we had acquired that we could not or did not want to take with us. We had no wish to make a fortune, nor any hope of doing so, but we had to be careful not to appear to favour some would-be purchasers more than others. It was not difficult to find people willing to buy our belongings, so what we did was to make a list of the items we were disposing of, and let people bid what they were prepared to pay for whatever it was they wanted. Then we had to inform them about who was getting what. It seemed to work reasonably well.

The only item of ours not readily available in Ahoada was the kerosene fridge, still working well enough despite its close encounter with the blancmange. The only customer for this was Reverend, and we managed to agree on a price that was satisfactory to both of us. Minor items we were glad to give away at this stage, and one day we became aware of a row of grinning children outside the verandah gate, hopefully chanting "*Osseetameeleekee, osseetameeleekee.*" It took us a while to realise that this was the closest they could get to "Ostermilk," and they were actually asking for some of the empty powdered milk tins that we would not need much longer. A few of them were lucky.

Greetings are an important feature of life in West Africa, and this includes not only arrivals but also farewells. One day Reverend's wife Jeanette came to visit us, and presented us with a fine carved ebony lion's head as a memento of our time in Ekpeye. We also had to go through the ritual of being farewelled by the local Baptist Association at a special Friday service at Orupata Baptist church. On this occasion the service was conducted by Reverend, who was able to use a mixture of Ekpeye and English so that everyone understood what was going on - at least until the heavens opened and virtually every other sound was drowned out by the torrents of rain. We also became sharply aware that the thatched roof of the church was in need of repair! To our astonishment and embarrassment, the Baptist Association presented us with the sum of thirty shillings in lieu of a carving, a huge amount in terms of the local economy, where the church collections consisted largely of pennies. Of course for cultural reasons we could not refuse, but neither could we feel that we had made anything like a contribution to the life of the church that deserved such a generous gift.

We also had to make our own farewells in the village, and after the service on our last Sunday Bob and Okpara escorted us around the village to do the honours. Mr. Ebeku, the councillor, was not at home, but we did find both Chief Alabi, the traditional leader of the village, and the family of Elijah, our landlord. After we had paid several months rent in advance, we had not seen much of him, but we had no reason to suppose that our tenancy had given him any cause for regret. Without us, the house would have been standing empty. On a quick final visit Peter had at last removed what remained of his furniture, and without it the house did seem rather empty, though we were relieved to see the furniture restored to its owner.

Although our time among the Ekpeye people was nearly over, we were constantly reminded how little we really knew of their culture. For instance Bob assured us that he always felt stronger in the morning if he bathed at night. We could find no rationale for this belief, either in terms of his worldview or of ours, but if bathing at night made him feel stronger next day, then we were happy for him. He also told us about one kind of snake that spits its venom rather than biting its victims. This habit, he assured us, arose from the snake's chewing pepper. The snake Bob was telling us about apparently likes to live in pepper plants, and this is presumably how the idea that it chewed pepper gained currency. Such a habit seemed rather improbable to us, but we were in no position to contradict Bob. We never saw such a snake and had no wish to do so, so we were unable to identify it, though from our snake book we wondered if it might be a black-necked cobra.

The riots in Northern Nigeria at the end of July were more serious than we realised, and more than a few people from the Eastern Region were killed. We were booked to fly out through Kano in the north, one of the main centres where riots had taken place, and in the absence of clear information, we continued with our plans. Although we were flying home, the bulk of our possessions had to go by sea, and that meant getting them to Port Harcourt. This was where Jo Scaggs proved extremely helpful. On our last Sunday, she called in to Orupata so that we could see whether our two drums and one trunk would go in the back of her short-wheelbase Land Rover. Next day we hired the local County Council lorry, and loaded everything including the fridge onto it. I went with the lorry while Glenys remained in the village doing a few final jobs. The fridge was delivered to Reverend's home, and our belongings to Jo's house. Finally I drove her Land Rover back to Orupata to collect Glenys and Helen and our remaining few odds and ends. The local children were much in evidence at our departure, and to my surprise, our last sight of them revealed that they were having fun destroying the two posts that had held up our laundry line. One of the posts was pretty wobbly by then anyway, but we would have expected that our neighbours could have made some use of the clothes line to reduce the risk from tumbu fly larvae. But bushes had sufficed for hanging wet clothes on for generations, so why bother to change?

Our hen had delivered a fairly regular supply of eggs during her last couple of weeks with us, and we had never steeled ourselves to eat her. When we left Orupata, she accompanied us as far as Jo's house, where we donated her to our gracious hostess. Obviously we could set no restrictions on her fate under new ownership, and from the way Jo's cook eyed her, she probably found her way to a pot before long - but at least not before we left.

On arrival at Jo's house Helen declared that it was "a yellow house." It was indeed painted yellow, but in Helen's vocabulary at that time, her comment was about more than colour: "yellow" was in fact the highest form of commendation she could bestow. In comparison with our temporary home in Orupata, Jo's house was very well appointed, and we enjoyed the unaccustomed touch of "yellow" luxury, such as running water. The day ended however on a much more anxious note. When the time came to put Helen to bed, we discovered that her much loved soft toys, Teddy and Larry the Lamb, were nowhere to be found. We hunted high and low, but to no avail. Fortunately Helen went to sleep quickly and did not appear to miss them. Where could they be? The only hope we had, and it seemed a very slim one, was that they might still be in the village. At the end of our packing, we were just throwing things we did not want out of the window, where there was no shortage of eager young hands to receive them. Could Helen have joined in what must have seemed to her like fun, and thrown out her precious toys?

Now that we were guests in someone else's home and did not have to worry about cooking and such routine matters, we had the whole of the next day to reorganise everything we wanted to send home into the smallest possible space. I went across to Reverend's house nearby, and got the fridge working for him. Jo made sure that our round of farewells continued, by inviting Reverend and Jeanette to join us for lunch, and Roy, Alicia and Gary for the evening meal. We also commissioned Seven to ask around in the village to see if Teddy and Larry could be found. For the second night, Helen did not appear to miss them. Did she know something we didn't? We dared not ask her.

The following morning I typed up a detailed list of the contents of our drums and trunk, and then set off in the Land Rover with Seven to drive to Port Harcourt. The vehicle was overloaded, the driver overtired, and the road in poor condition in the middle of the rainy season. With an upset tummy, I was not feeling at all well, and was glad to have Seven's company. For him it was a special treat as he had never been to Port Harcourt before. Some parts of the town, especially the area called Diobu, had a murky reputation. Reverend had told us of a young man he knew who had made a visit to the town, and stayed with relatives in Diobu. He did not return to Ahoada when expected, nor for several more days. When he did get back, his friends and relatives discovered that he had been the victim of a "pole thief." Such thieves would approach open windows during the night, and with the aid of a long pole would remove things from the room without entering it, and without waking the sleepers. This young man had been unlucky enough to lose his trousers this way while asleep, and had been unable to return home until he could beg, buy or borrow another pair.

Seven did not see much of Port Harcourt on this occasion, as we just delivered the goods to the shipping agency, and drove straight back to Ahoada. On the way back we had to go through a roadblock manned by armed policemen. They did not give us any trouble with our empty vehicle, but I was so glad that they had not been there when we had been on our way down with the vehicle full. To have had to unpack and repack all our goods at that stage would have been the last straw.

After returning to Jo's for a light meal, I had to take Seven back to Orupata, but by then it was raining and the Land Rover would not start without being pushed. Once I had delivered Seven, the same thing happened again, so my very last departure from Orupata was rather ignominious, needing to have a push start in a borrowed vehicle. Grateful though we were for the use of the Land Rover, I felt that I never wanted to drive one again. And I never have.

The great thing about that last visit however was that contrary to our expectations Seven had located Teddy and Larry the Lamb. They were in the possession of Enoch's little son Manager, and could hardly have been in better hands. We were able to negotiate a ransom, and Teddy and Larry were returned to a joyful Helen, distinctly grubbier but otherwise none the worse for their adventure. After being washed and hung up by the ears to dry, they were restored to a condition which, if not exactly pristine, was at least clean enough to be allowed to come into contact with Jo's sheets. That evening Roy and Alicia took us to their home for the evening meal, and as Enoch was now their night watchman, we were able to deliver the ransom to him – two little-used rubber squeaky toys. In all likelihood Manager found that toys which made a noise were a lot more fun than silent, threadbare soft toys. Whether Enoch would have agreed we did not stay to find out. Larry has since vanished into the mists of time, but a venerable if emaciated Teddy has survived to be passed down to endure the love of the next generation.

The day Seven and I went to Port Harcourt, an SIL member (another Ian) brought the VW van down from Enugu, collected the items we were selling or giving to Ian and Amelia, and went on to Abua to spend the night there with them. In the morning he returned to Ahoada with them so that they too could farewell us. Jo was going to Abua that day, so they returned home with her. We loaded up the VW and set off for Enugu, taking Bob with us. We had expected to stay a couple of nights at the SIL group house, but it turned out that someone there had hepatitis, and in view of Glenys' pregnancy it would have been rather risky for her to be unnecessarily exposed to the possibility of infection. So Maurice and Lorraine had kindly invited us to stay at their home instead. As it happened Lorraine was also expecting their second child. Their daughter Rosanne was a year older than Helen, and a regular chatterbox who kept us fully entertained during a short shopping expedition. While we were with Maurice and Lorraine, two carloads of people from Ika turned up, so we had the unexpected pleasure of seeing them again too.

We cleared up a few small administrative jobs at the SIL office and said goodbye to our friends there. Bob had accompanied us to Enugu with two goals in view. One was to do a little bit more work on transcribing the few remaining stories on the tapes, and the other was to see if there was any chance of getting a job. There was some building work planned at the SIL premises, and we wondered if he might have some part in it. Several SIL people had met him, and we were able to give him a good recommendation. Casual labouring work would not use all his abilities, but it would be better than nothing. However the work was not yet ready to begin and Bob would have to go home and wait a month or so before he knew whether he would get a job. We were sorry that we could not do more for him, but at least he had had a varied and unusual year with us that had expanded his horizons and provided him with more income than he would otherwise have had.

On a Saturday morning Maurice took us and Bob to the airport for our final departure. For Bob, it was a first visit to an airport, and for Helen and me it was to be our first ever commercial flight (Glenys had flown before we were married). While in the Air Training Corps at school, I had flown several times in small RAF planes, and had learnt that I was not one of the world's natural aviators, so I was a little apprehensive. Glenys had no such qualms, and in the event my anxiety proved unfounded. The aircraft was a Fokker Friendship, with wings set high on the fuselage to allow a good view from every window, and the flight to Kano via Kaduna was very smooth. There were only eight passengers on a 40-seater plane, so Nigeria Airways could hardly have made a profit on the flight. But we could move around freely and look out either side at will. The small number of passengers was a reflection of the political situation: people from the east were not flying to the north at that time. On its return, the plane probably had a heavier load.

Our connecting flight out of Kano did not leave till the following Monday, but as there was no flight from Enugu to Kano on Sunday we had no choice but to spend two nights there. We were put into the Central Hotel in Kano for one night at the airline's expense, though we had to pay for the second night ourselves. The hotel was quite expensive, so we ate as much as we could while the airline was paying, and economised when it wasn't. Helen was fascinated by the running water in the hotel, and whenever we had occasion to use a bath or washbasin she asked eagerly "Shall I put the flug (plug) in?" or "Shall I pull the flug out?" as appropriate. Up to this point her language world had been simple and consistent: black people spoke Ekpeye and white people spoke English. In Kano this neat division began to break down, as she quickly discovered that there were black people who did not speak Ekpeye. When we got to Greece, she was further disconcerted to find that there were white people who did not speak English. This was more disorientating for her than we realised, and for a few weeks her vocabulary seemed to stop growing.

On the Sunday morning we took a taxi to a church associated with the Sudan Interior Mission, and attended a well filled service. In the afternoon we took a taxi ride around the old city, and saw amongst other things the remains of the Igbo market that had been burnt down in the July riots. The old city, with its flat roofed houses, small doors and windows and dark alleys created quite a sinister impression on us, and we did not feel that Kano was a place we would choose to live in. One of the waiters in the hotel restaurant was a young Igbo man from the Eastern Region, and when he found out we had been living in the east, he was eager to talk to us about the unstable political situation. He told us that at the end of the month when he received his pay, he was intending to leave and return to his home in the east. Neither he nor we knew that at the end of the month there would be a third and even more bloody round of anti-Igbo rioting. When we heard about it, we wondered whether he had ever made it back home. There was no way to find out.

When Monday came the United Arab Airlines coach took us to the airport. We had no problems with the customs, and joined a not very full flight to Cairo on what was then a very modern jet plane, a Comet 4C. Although we had enjoyed our year in Nigeria and made many friends, it was not without some relief that we saw the dry and dusty terrain of the north drop away below us as the plane took off.

Chapter 17
Coda in Greece

The journey from Kano to Athens involved a connection in Cairo with a change of airline, and of course the journey from Kano to Cairo on United Arab Airlines was much the longer sector, well over four hours' flying. Helen approved of flying because sweets were given away liberally and frequently, and for her this was a new experience. Most of this flight sector was across the Sahara Desert, a hot, brown and very forbidding landscape, devoid of signs of human activity. Eventually the monotony was broken by a green streak from one horizon to the other – the Nile valley. There could be no more vivid illustration of the fact that essentially Egypt is the River Nile, and even after many hundreds of subsequent flights that sight remains one of the most impressive aerial views we have ever had.

Our connecting flight to Athens on Yugoslavian Airlines was delayed, and for some reason our checked-in baggage remained with us in the transit lounge rather than being automatically transferred to the next flight. It was on a trolley in the charge of a dejected little porter who followed us everywhere, mournfully muttering "Four pieces, four pieces," and clearly expecting a tip. But we had only a little Nigerian money and some Greek drachmas, neither of which were any use to him, so he had to go without his tip. We did not feel very sorry for him, as I could perfectly well have pushed the trolley around myself. More urgent to us was the fact that it was hot, and we were all getting thirsty. We had no Egyptian money to buy a drink with, and credit cards were still a thing of the future for us, but eventually we managed to persuade Yugoslavian Airlines to provide some drinks for us free of charge.

By the time the plane took off it was dark, so we could not see anything more. Whereas the cabin crew on the United Arab Airlines flight had been young and cheerful, and the food good, the Yugoslavian stewardesses were rather grim, military-looking matrons, and the food was regulation socialist rations. It was after 10 p.m. by the time we landed in Athens. We took an airline bus into town, then a taxi to the home of our friends Phaedon and Phopho. Their son Aimilios, a few months younger than Helen, was also eager to welcome us, though Helen was somewhat taken aback when he opened their acquaintance with a passionate kiss. Despite the late hour, they were all still awake, and more than ready to provide us with a delicious fruit salad of grapes, apples, water melon and peaches. Much as we had come to enjoy our standard village fruit salad of pawpaws, oranges, limes and bananas, it was wonderful to have a change. Helen was particularly partial to apples, which she could not remember having before. Not knowing the English word for them, she quickly acquired the Greek word, which she adjusted from *milo* to *bilo*, and had no hesitation in tacking on to the Ekpeye verb for "give me." "*Nem bilo*" was a sentence we heard frequently over the next two weeks, perhaps the first mixed Ekpeye-Greek sentence in the history of the world.

Though our journey from Nigeria to Greece had been long and had ended late, it had not involved a change of time zone, so we did not suffer from what is now called jet-lag. (This term was not around in those days, or if it was, was not yet widely used.) Nevertheless we all managed to sleep till half past nine next morning. When we woke up, Phaedon and Phopho had already gone out. We had a leisurely morning, and went for a walk in the afternoon with them and Aimilios. We learnt that like Glenys, Phopho was also expecting her second child, so our families were well matched. We discovered that in Greece, shopping hours were morning and evening, with shops closed during the afternoon heat, so we had what was then the new experience of evening shopping. We also quickly discovered that the intonation of Greek sentences is very different from English. When Phaedon and Phopho were chatting with each other in Greek, it often sounded to us as if they were quarrelling, though the wider context made it quite clear that they were not. As linguists we could only conclude that the intonation patterns that English people use when they are quarrelling are very close to the patterns that Greeks use for normal interaction. This is the kind of variation from which ethnic stereotypes develop. How Greeks speak when they really are quarrelling we did not have occasion to discover.

We had known Phaedon and Phopho when we (and indeed Amos) were all students together in England before any of us got married, and in fact I had shared a room with Phaedon for a year. He was always full of life, and full of mischief, and one of my clearest memories was of him trying to run up a down escalator somewhere on the Northern Line late one evening. (He did not succeed!) Now we had the chance to meet some other members of their families, not only all their parents, but also a brother and sister of Phopho's and a brother of Phaedon's. Both families had suffered from the vicissitudes of history. Phaedon's father's family had been among the many Greek refugees from Smyrna in Turkey in 1923, and had had to make new lives for themselves in Athens. It was no accident that the area of Athens where the refugees settled was given the name Nea Smyrne: New Smyrna. Phopho came from a large family, and during the hardships of the German occupation of Greece in the Second World War two of her siblings had starved to death. Hardly surprisingly, her mother had never really got over this tragedy.

Phaedon was the pastor of a small Protestant church in Athens, and Phopho was a speech therapist. Phaedon had reserved some of his annual leave for our visit, and we wanted to make the most of our time together. They had no car, and indeed no driving licences, so we decided that in order to have the greatest freedom of movement, I should hire a car. To do this I needed an international driving licence, which could have been a problem. At that time British driving licences had to be renewed annually, and we had been out of Britain for more than a year. However I did have a Nigerian driving licence that was still valid, and on the basis of that, the Greek authorities were willing to issue me with an international licence, so we were able to hire a VW Beetle. In the days before compulsory seat belts, this was quite roomy enough for four adults, two toddlers and two unborn babies.

Before we took out the car, we made a beeline for the Acropolis, which was within walking distance of Phaedon and Phopho's flat. 1966 was before the days of the Jumbo Jet and mass tourism, and incredible as it seems today, we were able to go inside the Parthenon and walk around there. My own undergraduate background was in Classics, but I had never had the opportunity to visit Greece before, so wandering about the Acropolis was like a dream come true. And of course we also visited the Areopagus, the hill below the Acropolis where according to the record of Acts 17 St. Paul had preached.

But the Beetle gave us the freedom to go further than our feet could carry us, and we made good use of it. The terrain in Greece could hardly have been more different from that of the Niger Delta. Instead of a flat, sandy, thickly forested country, we were in a mountainous, stony and relatively barren one. Instead of being surrounded by rivers and swamps, we were now never far from the sea, with broad beaches and rocky islets. The temperature was very little lower, but the air was free of the enervating humidity of the Niger Delta. We both felt so much more energetic than we had during the wet season in which we spent our last few months there.

The first day with the car we drove down to Cape Sounion at the south-eastern extremity of Attica. The famous Temple of Poseidon there was one attraction, but we also had our first swim in Greek waters, and were astonished at the range of fish that Phaedon's goggles revealed. Not only was the sea much clearer and warmer than the Bristol Channel where we had both spent childhood holidays, but the sun shone almost continuously and we never needed to worry about the possibility of rain.

The next day we visited Lake Marathon, a reservoir at the head of a gorge, set in lovely wooded country. Then we took an unsurfaced mountain road down to Marathon village to see the memorial to the Greek victory over the invading Persians in 490 B.C. That road gave us a slow puncture in one tyre, but we put some more air in and managed to get safely back to Athens to have a repair made. At Marathon for the first time in our lives we saw a fisherman who had caught an octopus preparing it for cooking - by bashing it on the quayside. This did nothing to encourage us to try eating octopus!

To my surprise Phaedon was rather concerned about my beard. As he explained, in Greece in those days the only men with beards were hippies and Greek Orthodox priests. Since I fell into neither category, he was not at all sure that I would make the right kind of impression on the members of his congregation when he took us to church. The beard had not been there for long, and I felt no emotional attachment to it, so I shaved it off, leaving only a moustache such as many Greek men sported. But I did not like the moustache, and it survived the beard by only a few days. The cultural implications of facial hair can change, however. On a visit to Greece a decade or so later, I noted that Phaedon had grown a moustache, and after another decade his own face was adorned by a beard. I smiled to myself, but said nothing.

After the church service, we drove a short distance outside Athens to the summit of Mount Parnes, which offered fine views down over the city. But the really memorable experience was the fragrance of the pine trees and the variety of wild herbs that grew there in profusion.

During my classical studies, it had been prescribed that we should read some "bucolic poetry," which celebrated the sights, sounds and smells of the countryside. I had never enjoyed that kind of poetry much, but the trip up Mount Parnes gave me some belated understanding of what the poets were inspired by. On the way there were a couple of village Orthodox churches that we stopped to visit. They were unlike any church we had been in before, highly decorated with wall paintings and icons, though as might be expected in a small rural church, the icons did not seem to be particularly good examples of their kind.

Another excursion required a very early start, and took us on an all-day trip to Delphi, the site of the most famous oracle in ancient Greece. We got out of the Athens traffic before eating, and had a picnic breakfast out in the country. In September the grapes were being harvested, and at one point we stopped to talk to some men who were loading masses of grapes onto the back of a lorry. To our surprise they invited us to help ourselves to as many grapes as we wanted, but even the six of us could make no visible difference to the huge heaps. The men had a donkey with them, and were very happy for us to put Helen on the donkey's back to take a photo. At another village where we stopped, Phopho was delighted to be able to buy a sheepskin at a much lower price than she would have paid in Athens. This she wanted to make a bed cover for Aimilios, and it was not until she got it home that she realised how dirty and smelly it was. However she persisted in soaking it in the bath for several days, and eventually it was deemed fit to serve its intended purpose.

After paying our respects to the impressively sited ruins of the ancient oracle at Delphi, we continued on down the hill to the village of Itea on the northern shore of the Gulf of Corinth where we enjoyed a quick swim and a meal of sprats and chips at an open-air café. It was a long and tiring drive back to Athens, and we could not escape the heavy evening traffic, but it had been a magnificently satisfying day.

Both the children were good eaters, and the day was rounded off with a meal at home, accompanied as usual by vigorous chatter. As we sat at table, Phaedon was occupied with supplying Aimilios with spoonful after spoonful of food while facing us and discoursing eagerly on some topic or other. We could see, as he could not, that although Aimilios was obediently opening his mouth for each new spoonful, he was not swallowing the food, but such was Phaedon's absorption in his subject that we could not get a word in to warn him. Eventually the inevitable happened, and a huge mouthful of food was joyfully strewn over Aimilios' bib and high chair. The resulting paternal displeasure was not entirely deserved!

The next day we took life much more easily, but our time with the Beetle was limited so we made one more long trip, this time into the Peloponnesus. With another early start we had breakfast by the Corinth canal, then went on to see the ruins at Mycenae, and ended up at a place called Tolon, where there was a sheltered bay with an idyllic sandy beach that offered our best bathing yet. The sky was cloudless, the sea really blue, the water pleasantly warm, and the fish plentiful and multicoloured. We enjoyed it so much there that we abandoned our original plan to visit the famous amphitheatre at Epidauros, and went no further, though on the way back we stopped to see the extensive ruins of ancient Corinth, including the place where St. Paul stood before the Roman governor Gallio according to Acts 18.

Since I was now inoffensively beardless, Phaedon invited me to speak to the members of his church about the work we had been doing in Nigeria. The idea of language study as a tool leading to Bible translation was something of a novelty for Greeks because they are the only people in the world who have always had the New Testament in their own language. By this time I had a bout of laryngitis, though as Phaedon had to interpret everything I said into Greek, he was the only person who needed to hear my words, and the event passed off satisfactorily.

However the day was marred by my putting a dent in the Beetle in parking it in a space that was not really big enough, but was the only space available anywhere near the church. Although the car was fine to drive on the open road, it was not easy to manoeuvre because both the front and rear bumpers stuck out a good deal further than could be seen from the driving seat. But when the time came to hand the car back, the hire car company did not seem to worry about the dent. Such was the panache (or recklessness, depending on your point of view) with which Greeks drove that hardly a car in Greece was without a dent, and they were regarded more as honourable battle scars than as undesirable damage. Greek drivers could be quite voluble in expressing their opinion of other drivers, both by words and by gestures. Although Phaedon himself did not drive at that time, he was quite ready to teach me some of the words and gestures favoured by Greek drivers. However, when on one occasion I was sufficiently provoked to use one of the gestures, he was horrified, and told me never to use it again.

In those days the Acropolis remained open late into the evening when it was full moon. The only explanation for this that we could get from our hosts was that Greeks were romantic. However from a window at the top of the stairs that led to their flat, one could see the Acropolis, and although a full moon occurred while we were with them, we spared ourselves the extra walk at the end of a tiring day, and were content with looking out of the window.

Once we had parted with the car we were able to make one more trip, this time by public transport. It involved a bus ride to the port of Piraeus and a 90-minute boat trip to the island of Aigina in the Saronic Gulf. It was a strange feeling to be sailing in waters where one of the most significant naval battles in European history had taken place, the battle of Salamis in which the Greeks defeated the second Persian invasion in 480 B.C. On Aigina we took a local bus across the island to Agia Marina where we indulged in more sea bathing and another beach picnic. This was our swan song in Greece, and using public transport made us all more grateful for the days when we had had the Beetle.

Next day, exactly fifteen months after we had left England, it was time to return. The return proved to be even less smooth than our departure had been. Phaedon and Phopho came with us on the bus to the airport in the morning, and there we said our farewells to them. To our dismay the BEA flight to London was seriously delayed and did not take off till after five o'clock in the afternoon. Entertaining a two-year old for an extra four hours without warning is not an easy task, but Helen slept for part of the time. The car we had ordered in Port Harcourt was supposed to be delivered to us on arrival at Heathrow, and we began to wonder whether the luckless driver would still be waiting for our plane. The delay was also unwelcome to the group of people who had come from Bristol to meet us at Heathrow, my parents and my brother, and Glenys' friend Kath. The plan was for my parents and brother to join us in the new car and drive down to Bournemouth, where Glenys' parents lived. Kath would return to Bristol on the bus. The delay was so long, however, that she had to give up and go home before we arrived, and thus had a wasted journey to the airport.

When at last we did arrive, we were happily reunited with the family, but there was no sign of the car. We paged for the driver a couple of times with no result. It was now late on a Saturday evening, and there was no possibility of contacting a Ford office to find out what had happened, and the chances of getting to Bournemouth on public transport were decreasing by the minute. Fortunately for us some friends of ours, Bill and Doreen Mason, lived near Heathrow in Hounslow. Bill was an engine fitter with BOAC, as it then was, and they had also come to meet us at the airport as a surprise. Seeing our predicament, they did not hesitate in inviting all of us to camp in their house overnight. With their car plus one taxi we all managed to get there. For them to pack four extra adults, a teenager and a baby into a three-bedroom house already occupied by themselves and a teenage son was no light task. Fortunately their older son was away, and somehow we all squeezed in, Glenys and I having Helen in the same bed with us. What would we have done without Bill and Doreen? Their younger son Brian for some reason was out late and was unaware that his home had been invaded by an unexpected gang of aliens, so his mother had to leave little notes here and there for him warning him not to go into certain rooms because people were sleeping in them! I cannot remember whether his own bedroom was out of bounds, but he was a natural extrovert, and took it all in good part when the explanation was forthcoming next day.

In the morning we were able to get down to Bournemouth by train, though even that relatively simple journey was not without incident. There had been a derailment at Micheldever, and we had some delay there, but nothing to rival the efforts of BEA. In Bournemouth we settled in with Glenys' parents while my parents and brother were installed in a nearby guest house. At last Helen had met all the grandparents whose photos she had become familiar with in Orupata.

Within a few days we were able to sort out the car problem with Ford. It appeared that after we had left Orupata, the agent in Port Harcourt had tried to contact us with some bureaucratic query or other, but of course had been unable to do so. Accordingly the order for the car had not been processed, and the company had not been able to get in touch to inform us. They did however provide another vehicle for us to use until the car we had ordered was delivered a couple of weeks later. All that remained was for us to find somewhere to live. Since I had to concentrate on writing a thesis, I no longer needed to go to SOAS every day. Thus it proved possible for us to live in Christchurch, not far from Glenys' parents, and for me to travel to London about once a fortnight. In this way I got used to being a post-graduate student again, but of a rather different kind from before and at a new stage of study.

Chapter 18
Epilogue

Once we were settled in Christchurch, life took on a more normal English pattern. While we were no longer in Nigeria, Nigeria was constantly with us as I slowly analysed all the stories we had recorded. In one respect Nigeria was with us in an unwelcome way. On return home, we all had routine health checks at the Hospital for Tropical Diseases in London. Glenys and Helen were declared fit, but there was some question whether I had contracted bilharzia, an unpleasant worm-borne disease. I had to go into the hospital for a few days for further investigation, and by then it was perilously near to Christmas. It was an unusual hospital environment in that none of the patients were really ill. Like me, most were simply under investigation. Indeed several of them made an unauthorised excursion to Covent Garden with some of the nurses early one morning to buy Christmas trees to decorate the ward with. I had visions of being incarcerated for the holiday, but eventually I was declared free of infection and allowed to return home.

There remained a lot more work than I had realised for me to do before I could submit my thesis. Our new baby daughter entered the world safely in January 1967, and was followed by another one sixteen months later. Welcome as these events were, they did not speed up the writing of the thesis but eventually the task was completed, and our long-term goal was accomplished.

We had always known that our time among the Ekpeye people would be limited and short, but we had hoped that when we left somebody else would be able to continue the work we had begun, and eventually translate at least the New Testament into Ekpeye. This happened in Abuan and Engenni, but for various complex reasons it did not happen in Ekpeye, and has still not happened. Now there is a challenge waiting for someone...

At home we had time to reflect on how our year in Africa had affected us. We had not gone there with any illusions about changing the world, but the African world had certainly changed us. On the level of our Christian experience, we had been brought into contact with people from various church traditions different from our own, and had learned to appreciate them, and to recognise the grace of God at work in their lives. On the cultural level, we had not only seen a very different kind of lifestyle, but had to some degree participated in it.

Perhaps the most important thing was that we had acquired a new perspective on the things we had always taken for granted in England, especially running water and electricity. We had found that with a willingness to learn new ways of doing things one could get by perfectly well without them. It might take a bit longer, and could sometimes be frustrating, but it could be done. We had also found that we were not always as willing to learn as we might have been!

We had also come to realise that people were still people, even if their value systems and ways of doing things were different from anything we had encountered before. They may have lacked many of the opportunities for medical care and education that we regarded as normal, but they had the same kind of hopes and fears as we did, and the same kind of love for their children. Their lives were not as cluttered with possessions as ours, but probably they had a better perception of the value of human relationships than we did. Their expectations from life were lower than ours, and this probably gave them a greater resilience in the face of misfortune than we would have shown. And they would need all of this in the tragic years of the Biafra conflict that was already looming, and began a few months after our departure.

By the time that war was over, our lives had moved in a very different direction, and took us to south east Asia. We never again lived in a village situation, and perhaps were never again so closely engaged with an alien culture. We certainly never again lived in such a demanding climate, but the lessons we had learnt in Orupata stood us in good stead as we were called upon to adapt to other cultures. As it turned out, we have never returned to West Africa, much less to Orupata, but we have good reason to be grateful to the people there who made us welcome in their midst and tolerated our eccentricities even though few of them could have had much understanding of the purposes behind our stay. They gave us much more than we could have given them, and this record of our stay is a small way of saying a belated "thank you: *mekane-oo*."

"Interaction is a two-way dynamic;
it should not be thought of
purely in terms of European acting upon African;
both sides clearly act upon each other."

(Niall Finneran, *The Archaeology of Christianity in Africa.*
Stroud: Tempus, 2002, page 149.)

Appendix:
Tortoise and the Princess

Many of the folk tales that we recorded had Ọkwụlụkwọ the Tortoise as their hero (or villain, depending on the story). Some of their motifs were already familiar from a childhood book of Brer Rabbit stories. This was hardly surprising as these stories had originated in West Africa. In my thesis I gave a detailed analysis of one of the stories to illustrate the grammatical structures of Ekpeye in so far as I had been able to analyse them. It seems appropriate to finish this book by repeating this story. If western logic played any part in folk tale cycles, this should be the last story in the series, but such considerations played no part in the minds of the Ekpeye story tellers. Usually Tortoise is presented as the underdog trickster who comes out on top, but this story was one of the small number where he gets his comeuppance, this time at the hands of Ewu the Grasscutter (a large bush rodent). I have not used the translation given in my thesis, but have prepared a fresh one, which I hope will be a little easier for readers who do not know the Ekpeye to follow.

Once upon a time, Ọkwụlụkwọ the Tortoise went hunting in the forest. While he was hunting, he searched and searched for game, but couldn't find any. At last he saw a spot where he thought there was an animal, and fired his gun. When he got to the spot, it turned out that it was a princess that he had shot dead. So he picked her up, and hid her up a tree.

Next day, he said to Ewu the Grasscutter, "Let's go hunting."

"Come on then," replied Ewu.

Ọkwụlụkwọ told Ewu, "You go this way and I'll go that way. As you go, if you see a troop of monkeys, you shoot." Ewu agreed, so off they went.

When they reached the right place, Ọkwụlụkwọ went and shook the branches where he had tied the princess, and Ewu fired at the spot. Then Ọkwụlụkwọ said, "Oh my goodness! You've gone and killed a princess! You're as good as dead." Ewu was in great distress, and ran all the way home.

When he got home, he dressed up in clothes that were very smart, then went back to the place where he and Ọkwụlụkwọ had been. When he and Ọkwụlụkwọ met, Ọkwụlụkwọ said to him, "You're very smart, considering you've just killed a princess!" Then Ewu told Ọkwụlụkwọ that her father the chief had made him welcome, and that he was the one who had bought the clothes for him, and told him that he had been wanting to kill his daughter anyway. So the two of them had done well.

When Ọkwụlụkwọ got home, he thought about the matter, then ran off to the chief's house, and told the chief, "I was the one who killed that person only yesterday, but you went and rewarded Ewu."

"Who was it you killed?" asked the chief.

"I shot your daughter dead, the one you said you wanted to kill anyway."

"Ah!" said the chief, "So you were the one who did it! And I was wanting to kill her indeed!" Then the chief had Ọkwụlụkwọ locked up. The chief was furious over the affair, so he had Ọkwụlụkwọ executed.

When he killed him, Ọkwụlụkwọ had no excuse to make at all.